BRIDGEVILLE ELEMENTARY

A BIG HISTORY

OF A SMALL SCHOOL

Virginia Howard Mullan
Original edition, 2024, 978-1-7373675-8-1
Reprint edition, 2025, 978-1-962081-37-5

Design by Virginia Howard Mullan and Mia Costales
Layout by Mia Costales

The Press at Cal Poly Humboldt
Cal Poly Humboldt Library
1 Harpst St.
Arcata, CA 95524-8299
press.humboldt.edu

Front Cover: Bridgeport School circa 1889.
Back cover: Top: Marvin, Muriel "Sis," and Kenneth Stapp; June Zeron and Roy Sibley at Showers Pass Graduation in 1928. Photo courtesy of Rowetta Miller. Bottom: Mrs. Brandt's second and third grade class from 1955.

BRIDGEVILLE ELEMENTARY

A BIG HISTORY

OF A SMALL SCHOOL

THE *What Remains* SERIES

BY

VIRGINIA HOWARD MULLAN

Facing page, clockwise: 1988 Humboldt County Science Fair t-shirt; Bridgeville Blazers t-shirt; 1989 Humboldt County Olympics of the Mind t-shirt; Bridgeville School Reading Club t-shirt; Pam Walker, Bridgeville School cook, student counselor advisor & PTA president and Dana Johnston, maintenance man bus driver, life science teacher and pottery teacher; History Day t-shirt; homemade rainforest in Barry Blake's classroom; varsity volleyball team; Bridgeville students demonstrating tetrahedron kites they made; varsity volleyball team and Bridgeville alumni; Mike Grady and Mark Middleton at the Renaissance Fair on the playground; Bridgeville Blazers t-shirts.

The math team pictured in front of a piece of P.E. equipment called a "stegel." Back row (left to right): Jacob Middleton, Kyle Ritter, Leah Sheline, Tonde Razooly. Middle: Alice Hess, Monica Little, Barry Barnwell, Yana Sweeney, Heidi Day, Daniel Bywater. Front row: Samantha Gray, Ryan Samuelson.

1988 HUMBOLDT COUNTY SCIENCE FAIR

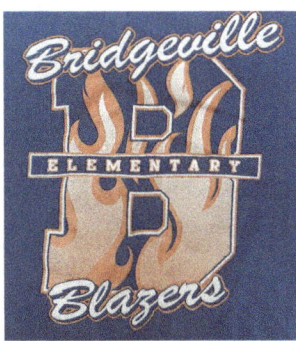

Bridgeville ELEMENTARY Blazers

1989 HUMBOLDT COUNTY OLYMPICS OF THE MIND

BRIDGEVILLE BLAZERS

BRIDGEVILLE BLAZERS

Bridgeville School Reading Club

MAY California 2002 I ♥ HD History Day in California

The entrance to Bridgeville Elementary circa 1999 before Mr. Mullan and the School to Career kids built the new Bell Tower to house the original school.

The Bell Tower Dedication from left to right: Lola Cathey, former teacher/administrator; Jessie Wheeler former school board member; Eleanor May long time resident; in the background Lori Sheline former teaching assistant; Corinne Fearrien former teacher; John Blakely teacher/administrator.

CONTENTS

The abbreviations LIB and LIC are used if the information is known. LIB is an abbreviation for lapses into Bridgeville Elementary School District; which means when the school closed those children and that area became part of the Bridgeville Elementary School District. LIC for lapses into Cuddeback School District.

Leah Sheline, Ms. Mullan and Alice Hess between the "old library" (on the left-actu-
ally the third library, the first was a shelf in the one-room schoolhouse; the second was
beneath the bell tower page 18) which was also Ms. Mullan's classroom for two years
before she moved to the classroom on the right at the end of the "portable/temporary"
classrooms built after the 1978 fire. This library was torn down to make way for the
new wing which would have the breezeway. When Ms. Mullan moved to the new
wing, Ms. Fearrien moved into the brown classroom on the right where she taught
for many years. The old bus barn is in the background, as is the original location of
the first sea-train that Bridgeville School purchased; which is next to the playground.
The "new" gym and the "old" locker room are behind the photographer. The flagpole
between the library porch and the brown portable is the same flagpole by which Ms.
Brandenburg and her class buried a time capsule circa 1964. The fourth library was
in a truly temporary room on the asphalt where the basketball courts currently are.
Another temporary classroom was adjacent to it and the kids had to walk through the
library to get to their class. That was a challenging year for librarian Marylin Grady!
The fifth and current library is in the new wing.

ACKNOWLEDGMENTS

I'd like to thank the many friends and acquaintances who shared their stories of Bridgeville School with me, helping to create a more robust representation of the Bridgeville School through the years.

Thanks to Mendie Ballester and Humboldt County Office of Education for the pictures of one room school houses of Larabee, Showers Pass, Burr Creek, and others. Thanks to Colby Smart, Ed.D. the Deputy Superintendent of Humboldt County Office of Education who allowed me to use the archived issues of the Bulletin Board and taught me about Emergency Schools in Humboldt County.

Thanks to Jessica Springer, over the years, for allowing me to access old P.T.A. notes and other goodies in the archives. Her enthusiasm and encouragement for this project are much appreciated!

Thanks to Jessie Wheeler for helping me read cursive names and knowing how to spell many "old time" Bridgeville names. Her enthusiasm, many Facebook messages, delightful conversations, generosity in sharing her time, photos, primary sources and connections helped me immensely. Our conversations about Bridgeville have always been a source of entertainment for me. I especially appreciated her searching out errors in the prerelease edition.

Thanks to William C. May for his generous sharing of photos and memories. I'm grateful for his suggested revisions.

Thanks to George Brightman for allowing me to look through all his photo albums!

Thanks to Rowetta Miller for all her information on Showers Pass and Heart's Valley School, and typing at 5 a.m. I appreciated her copy editing of the proof edition.

Thanks to Lauri Rose for looking over and discussing my "original" manuscript. Thanks to Sue Gordon and Susan Rogers for their friendship and discussing the Van Duzen Schools with me. Thanks for connecting me to Peggy Canale. Thanks to Peggy Canale for sending me a copy of her booklet on the history of the Van Duzen Schools.

Thanks to Peg Wheeler and Dottie Simmons for their friendship and assistance in determining mile markers on Highway 36. Without them I wouldn't have figured out where the Van Duzen Emergency School was.

Thanks to Charlie at Humboldt County Historical Society for scanning photos for this project (and others).

Thanks to Phoenix Orr for typing up most of Appendix 12.

Thanks to Kyle Morgan, the Scholarly Communications and Digital Scholarship Librarian at Cal Poly Humboldt.

Thanks to Mia D. Costales for going through this edition with a fine tooth comb and always being amenable and supportive to my suggested additions.

Thanks to the Patreon supporters, listed on the next page, whose donations allowed for pictures to be purchased for this endeavor from the Humboldt County Historical Society and Diana Schoenfeld. Together we donated over $200.00 to the Humboldt County Historical Society for this project.

Thanks to the many students & staff at Bridgeville who made working there a "really good time," (most days) and their friendship through the years.

Thanks to my family for being a constant source of joy in my life.

The morning after our retirement party 2015.

THANK YOU
PATREON SUPPORTERS

Becky Howard Burmeister
Jordan Collings
Paul Mullan
Denise Howard
Paul W. Howard
Mike Paul
Mike Mullan
Gina Montagna
Michaelyn Howard Mullan
New Xiong
Jessie A.Wheeler

Urso Chappell
Chelcie Mullins
Matt Breece
Dustin Wiesner
Patty Kendrick
Margaret Kay Guy
Nadya Klingel
JoJo Brazil
Daniel Wylder Mendez
Darci Diage

BEFORE PATREON

Julia Park Howard & C. Ward Howard
inspired me to follow my dreams.
Art Martin and Theo Johnson
encouraged me to keep writing.

Thanks to Mike Mullan for his unending support of me...
and all my ventures.

I am so very grateful for each and every one of you!

  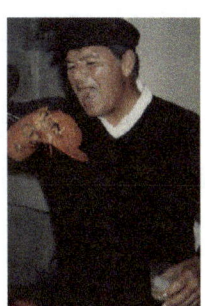 

From left to right: Ward & Judy Howard, Mike Mullan, Art Martin and Theo Johnson.

PREFACE

I taught at Bridgeville School for 31 years. I was hired as a fourth/fifth grade combination class teacher. The next year I was assigned to the fifth/sixth grade. That's how it started, I was excited to have a job and to be teaching kids, as they taught me. I fell in love with the place. But I wasn't the only one. Something about Bridgeville and the surrounding forests, provokes nostalgia. Evelyn Schuster Worthen taught at Bridgeville from 1932-1936, only a few years. Yet, it so captured her heart that she wrote a book during the sunset of her life entitled *The Unfolding Drama of Bridgeville*; for which I was interviewed.

There were some inaccuracies in Evelyn's account which I noticed (at the time I was incensed by those errors, including my name being misspelled. Now I am much more forgiving of her mistakes and anyone else's after putting this project together).

Jessie Wheeler noticed Evelyn's errors as did Gloria and Philo Barnwell. The four of us, at different times, talked about the written historical record that needed to be righted. So, Jessie and I eventually decided to create a book about the history of Bridgeville which would right the misinformation in Evelyn's book and give a more in-depth look at both Bridgeville and the area around Bridgeville. (Scheduled to come out fall of 2026.)

COVID-19 and "sheltering in place" caused Jessie and I to veer off track for a few years; but in the spring of 2023, we had the bones of a 270 page book. The bad news was... over 80 of the pages were about the school and I wasn't even finished with that section yet. When the all-class reunion for Bridgeville School was planned for August 17, 2024, I thought, "Wouldn't it be nice to have a little pamphlet that everyone who came could take home."

Well, that didn't happen.

What did happen is what you are holding in your hands at this moment. This is not a work of writing that is to be read from the beginning to the end. It is for those of us, like Audrey Campbell, who only attended Bridgeville School for a short time but wanted to recapture those years in her 90s.[1] It is for teachers and students bitten by the nostalgia bug that want to revisit the school, (like Sean Byrd in 2024 or Mary Brandenburg (Jardin) in 1999) but don't have the time or means. The book is in chronological order so that the reader may turn quickly to what interests them. My hope is that this book will trigger echoes of the past. That the reader will experience memories so thick, they'll have to swat them away.[2]

The challenge is: there is always another story. When I add an earlier memory into the project (e.g. Albert Hunt's two lines from an interview from several years ago) it will change all the page layouts and typesetting that come after the inserted quote. It changes all the page numbers and references. I have one filing cabinet full of Bridgeville information including pictures, newsletters, practically anything you can think of, that has been collected for this project. Synthesizing it simultaneously was beyond my capabilities. So, there was a very back and forth through time that occurred as information became available. More information exists than can reasonably be included. Culling is the challenge... but Albert Hunt is going in, so a two line quote will take more than an hour to insert.

Because there is "always another story," some of them aren't here. Regrettably, I never did connect with Allan Baird, although I still hope to. That isn't the only information left out of this volume. Everyone who attended Bridgeville School or worked at Bridgeville School has additional stories to tell.

I have enjoyed researching the history of Bridgeville School, delighted in seeing the names of relatives of people I know and reliving memories of times spent there. I hope you find something of interest between these pages and that it brings you joy.

—Virginia Howard Mullan

INTRODUCTION

The purpose of *Bridgeville Elementary: a Big History of a Small School* is to convey a sense of what Bridgeville School was like over the years, from 1866-2023.

The teachers of Bridgeville and other schools are listed in chronological order and create the main skeleton this book. Early 20th century students are listed if that information is available. Rural Supervisors, the equivalent of a school superintendent, are listed if known. They usually covered several small schools, lived elsewhere, and generally only visited the schools six times per year. In later years, when Bridgeville School published staff lists which included support staff in addition to teachers then those personel are listed as well.

If there is a blank, e.g. the 1911-1912 school year, that means that there was no verifiable information found by the author for that year. Sometimes the teaching assignment next to a teacher's name is blank for the same reason, e.g. Robert Erwin.

If there is a year with two names and no additional information (such as in the Shower's Pass section 1906 Maude G. Smith and Frances E. Hood); that is all the information I have. I don't know if they taught during different seasons or sessions (my hunch) or if they taught together. Much of that information came from the *History of Humboldt County Schools* published by the Humboldt County Office of Education. If I was unable to augment that information with other sources, that is all we have.

As this project evolved, information on two "emergency schools" emerged which lapsed into Bridgeville School District. Lapsing into a school district means that when a small school closed those children and that area became part of a larger existing school district.

Emergency Schools were established in order to provide elementary education for children residing in the county or in order to provide elementary education for children of migratory laborers engaged in seasonal industries within the county. The county superintendent of schools may, with the approval of the county board of education, establish and maintain one or more emergency elementary schools for children. These emergency schools often didn't last long and the paperwork on them was often destroyed once they were part of Bridgeville School District. The emergency schools, that I am aware of, which eventually lapsed into Bridgeville School District were: Bridgeville Emergency School and Van Duzen Emergency School. Redwood Emergency School lapsed into Cuddeback School District.

This book is a work in process. As soon as more eyes are upon it, I'm sure that details will become more accurate and perhaps other opinions will be voiced. The contact information at the beginning of the book is real. I look forward to additional information or stories readers might send. I will incorporate what I can in future renditions of the *Bridgeville Elementary: A Big History of a Small School*.

A Bridgeville School Constitution Float in the Fortuna Parade in the late 1980's. I couldn't find the picture of Lisa Fiddler who is beautifully dressed and sitting on a shawl on the hood of the GMC, waving to the crowd. There is a quilting bee on the tailgate, Betsy Ross sewing a flag and some "Founding Fathers" signing the Declaration of Independence. Left to right, Jessica Gatlin, Barry Barnwell, Crystal Remmington, John Shafer, Shannon Dresen, Jason Hoopes and Kyle Ritter.

1

GITEL & THE NONGATL
PRIOR TO 1800

Gitel is the Sinkyone Indian name for Bridgeville.
—Dennis W. Turner, 1993

Before there was a "Humboldt County" there were people, living in the area we now call Bridgeville, educating their children in their culture and way of life. We take these pages to acknowledge those who have lived on and cared for the land from time immemorial. I want to express my gratitude to those who reside here, and to honor the Indigenous people who have lived and worked on and cared for this land historically and presently. I would encourage all to gain a deeper understanding of their history. When whites arrived in the Gitel area around the 1850's it was the beginning of an erasing of what came before. If one white man was killed, then six Native Americans were killed as compensation, as in the Drinkwater episode.

The Coyote Flat Murders in 1925, by Showers Pass, of Carmen Wagner and Henry Sweet were blamed on Jack Ryan a young Indigenous man who was convicted and sent to prison. Jack Ryan was later exonerated and posthumously pardoned in 1996.[3] Atrocities piled on atrocities. The most current episode the author heard about in this area was in 1972 when an Indigenous man was "strung up" to be hung in the bar next to the Dinsmore Store. Luckily some cooler heads intervened. But, that wasn't always the case.

The Nongatl were eradicated early in the history of Bridgeville. Nongatl villages were located along the Van Duzen River, the Upper Mad River, and the creeks that drained into those rivers. There were at least 35 villages. One of the large villages was located where the Cal Fire station is just beyond Brown's Creek.[4] The locals called the place "Diggers' Flat" and the people "Digger Indians" (a derogatory term) because of the colonizer's perception of Nongatl digging in the dirt (possibly collecting acorns from oaks). Other accounts refer to this area as "Indian Camp." The name Nongatl is a Hupa word meaning Athabaskan to the south. The following is from a 2009 article in the

North Coast Journal discussing Native Americans prior to arrival of white settlers.

"We are taught today that a 'tribe' called the Nongatls ranged over the entire drainages of both the Van Duzen River and Larabee Creek. However, interviews (some now a hundred years old) with [American] Indians born near the time of the whites' arrival indicate that there were actuality at least 15 separate tribal groups, each with its own name and territory, that lived in this vast area. These groups were so heavily attacked and their surviving members so widely dispersed that they ceased to exist as tribal units.

But there are [American] Indians today who can, for example, trace their ancestry to the Kittel tribal group, which occupied the Van Duzen River near Bridgeville, just as there are those who are connected with other groups, such as the Lolangkoks and the Nekannis, whose names most of us have never heard. Many of these [American] Indians are affiliated with the Bear River Band of the Rohnerville Rancheria, a federally recognized tribe with members who trace their ties to southern and eastern Humboldt County."

—*North Coast Journal*
Honor the History
article Oct. 15, 2009

It is appropriate for us to take a moment and be conscious of all that came before to lead us to this moment in time. I gratefully acknowledge the Native Peoples on whose ancestral homeland the Bridgeport School, Bridgeville School and all the other little schools were built. I appreciate the diverse and vibrant people who make their homes here today.

2

BRIDGEPORT & BRIDGEVILLE SCHOOLS

Bridgeport School circa 1889.

The first school out at Bridgeport (later called Bridgeville) was a private school taught by G. W. Norman who came into Humboldt County with us in 1866. I attended school there when I was about 14. [1869] Mr. Norman kept school at what is known as Indian Camp on the flat near Bridgeville [see page 1 for more information on Indian Camp]. There was not a school house, but we had school out of doors under the trees. Necessarily, this was a summer affair.

—George Friend Jr.[5]

1873
 Miss Cook was teaching in the Robinson Home without any sanctioning or support from Humboldt County.

May 7, 1875

Bridgeport School District was established by Humboldt County. Bridgeport School will eventually lapse into Bridgeville School District, but not until 1891. Between 1887 and 1891 there was some overlapping of the names and reporting to the Humboldt County Office of Education. The first school was located on a flat near the base of Schoolhouse Peak, later known as the Goat Rock area, approximately mile marker 22.4 on Highway 36. Some evidence suggests that the school was located at another locale on the Robinson Ranch before finally settling in its present location at Bridgeville where township sections 11, 12, 13 and 14 meet.

1876

Mr. S.A. Kneeland, teacher (the second year of the **Bridgeport District**). His salary was $75.00 a month. The furniture was inadequate. There were twenty-one boys and eleven girls in class. Water was available, but at a distance. No outhouse was available.[6]

1877

S. A. Kneeland, teacher - **Bridgeport.** Fifteen boys and nine girls were in class. There were now 11 books in the library.[7] Both the official Bridgeport School and an unofficial Bridgeville School were in operation at an unverified location. There was no recorded nearby water source for the Bridgeport School.

1877

Jane N. McNut, teacher - **Bridgeville.** Her salary was $70.00 a month. She taught seventeen boys and ten girls in kindergarten through grade eight. The furniture was reported as being inadequate. The ventilation was "very fair." There was an adequate supply of water, but it was ¼ of a mile away and the water supply dwindled in the autumn to almost nothing. There were 11 books in the library.[8]

Old Robinson ranch house just off Kneeland Road. Facing east with Rich Hunt ridge in background. Photo Courtesy of William May.

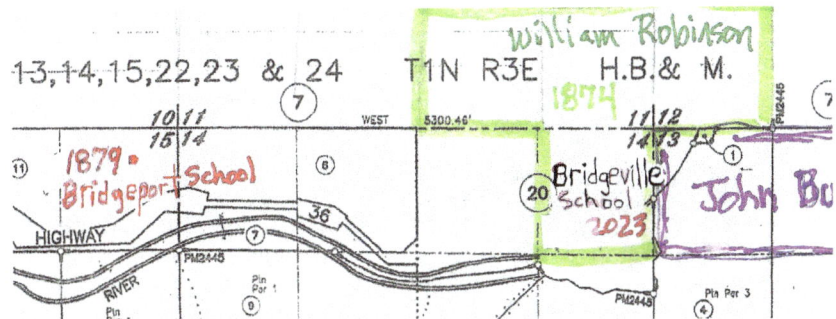

The coordinates of Bridgeville School.

May 20, 1879

William Slaughter Robinson sold Bridgeport School just over an acre of land in the northeast quadrant of the northeast section of section #15 in Township one North, range three east, for $1.00. This sale was certified by W. Webster, Justice of the Peace at the request of John Monroe. Currently Bridgeville School sits at the corner of 11/12/13/14.[9]

May 4, 1877

John J. Hale, then owner of **Bridgeport**, requested and received a post office designation and it was found that there was another Bridgeport in California so the name of the post office and town became Bridgeville.

1878

E. D. Daugherty, first term July to Nov. teacher - **Bridgeport/Bridgeville**. This is one of the duplicate records that makes it unclear if it is refering to Bridgeport School or Bridgeville School. The confusion is enhanced since the name of the town was changed in the prior year and people might have started calling Bridgeport School Bridgeville School. Whichever school it was...there were twenty-one boys and thirteen girls. Mr. Daugherty reported that the furniture was in fair condition. The water supply dwindled to almost nothing. There was still no outhouse.[10] Mr. Daugherty also taught at Iaqua School

1879

Carrie Williams, first term teacher - **Bridgeport.** James Fablinger second term teacher. Both Ms. Williams and Mr. Fablinger received $70.00 per month. Attendance during the different terms varied. There were between eleven and fifteen boys with six to eight girls. The number of books in the library rose to 35. During the second term James Fablinger was hired to replace Carrie Williams. Mr. Fablinger had experience teaching other places in Humboldt County. There still wasn't an outhouse.

Ellen Brown Fablinger, age 9.

James Fablinger was married to Ellen Brown January 23, 1876; the youngest daughter of Harper Ferry's John Brown and Mary Brown.[11] There is evidence that Ellen and James at some time, probably before teaching in Bridgeville, lived with Ellen's mom Mary in the big house at the intersection of Church and Brown Streets in Fortuna.[12] The Brown family was full of spunk and Ellen was no exception. Stories were reported about her and although there is controversy about the authenticity of this story, it gives you a flavor for the personality of Mr. Fablinger's wife. From the Eureka Standard, January 30, 1876. Ellen was born September 25, 1854; so in 1876 when she was 22 she was visiting Rohnerville. A man "noticed her coming along the sidewalk and commenced to sing 'John Brown's body lies a moldering in the grave'. The new Mrs. James Fablinger said nothing and when within reach of the insulter, dealt him a blow" which according to the Eureka Standard reporter the struck man "will remember this incident the rest of his life and he will take pains not to insult another lady."[13]

James Fablinger wasn't John Brown's only relative to teach at Bridgeville School, Lola Marie Cathey, John Brown's great, great granddaughter would not only teach at Bridgeville School, but also become the principal superintendent. Lola Cathey was one of the first women superintendents in Humboldt County.[14]

February 3, 1880

The **Bridgeville School District** was established by Humboldt County.

1880

Dan P. Albee, second term teacher - **Bridgeport School**. Mr. Albee was paid $70 per month. He was single and 24 years old. 13 boys and 13 girls attended Bridgeport. Water was still ¼ of a mile away. The size of the building was 16' by 24' with a 9' ceiling. There were four windows, two on each side of the building. There was still no outhouse.

Bridgeville School in the early 1900s.

In the 1880 census there is a 25 year old man named Jacob H. Wood who is listed as a boarder in Bridgeville with an occupation as teacher, but he isn't on the lists of Bridgeville or surrounding areas as a teacher.

1881

Dan P. Albee - **Bridgeport School.** $75.00 per month. 10 boys and 26 girls.

In the early years of Bridgeville and Bridgeport Schools the County Office of Education reported the years as just one year, i.e. 1881. Currently we refer to the school year from fall to spring: i.e. the 2024-2025 school year. Darlene Whiting explained how the weather, circa 1937, influenced the school year. "We had school all summer, except for one or two weeks around the 4th of July. In the winter, school closed down for all of December and January and sometimes part of November or February, depending on the weather."[15]

1882

Bridgeport School. The building was reported as 16' by 20' with a 9' ceiling compared to 1880's report which makes one wonder if there was a new building, a different measuring method or sloppy paperwork. No teacher listed.

1885

Trustees of Bridgeport School record a deed in Book 17 of Deeds page 799, allowing for water rights from Burns or Hoaglin Creek.

1887

W.L. Pedrick - **Bridgeport School & Bridgeville School**. Another duplicate entry so we are not sure which school. Mr. Pedrick's salary was $75.00 a month in 1887 and was raised to $80.00 a month in 1888. There were 11 grammar schoolers and 22 primary children in his class. Around the turn of the 20th century, grammar schoolers referred to children ages 10–14, while primary or elementary age students referred to children ages 5–9. It is hard to believe Mr. Pedrick some days had 36 children in class with only 12 desks reported. (There were 36 students reported in Bridgeport alone in 1881). There was water available, but there was no pump. His report says the building was 24' by 36' with a 16' ceiling with six windows and two doors (this is the approximate size of the old Bridgeville School that was still extant in 1984-even though this description is in Mr. Pedrick's Bridgeport report). There were 390 books in the library in 1887 but that number dropped the following year to 251. Two outhouses were provided.

1888

W.L. Pedrick - **Bridgeport School & Bridgeville School**. Another duplicate entry in the History of Humboldt County Schools. Both schools would report they had 390 library books.

1889-1890

Rufus Crippen - **Bridgeport School & Bridgeville School**. His salary was $75.00 a month. There were 6 boys and 10 girls in class. The building was 25' by 31 feet and a 14 foot ceiling. The Library had 328 books. There was no water available. There were two outhouses; one was good, but the other was not. There were 328 library books reported.[16]

April 13, 1891

The **Bridgeport School District** is "lapsed" into **Bridgeville School District**.

The year of this Bridgeville School photo is unknown, but it seems to be the building described by Mr. Pedrick in 1887 and Rufus Crippen in 1889 and used until 1984.

The teachers of Bridgeville School are listed on subsequent pages in chronological order and create the main skeleton of the rest of this chapter. Early 20th century students are listed if that information is available. Rural Supervisors, the equivalent of a school superintendent, are listed if known. They usually covered several small schools, lived elsewhere, and generally only visited the schools six times per year. In later years, when Bridgeville School published staff lists which included support staff in addition to teachers then those personel are listed as well.

Three sisters, the daughters of William Slaughter Robinson and Lovina Electa Albee, became Bridgeville School teachers. Caltha Robinson (the oldest), Gertrude Robinson and Bertha Robinson (the youngest). Their sister-in-law (who married their only brother William Albee Robinson) also taught at Bridgeville before she was married, seen in this list as Florence Knowles. Bertha went on to become Humboldt County's Superintendent of Schools in the early 1900s.

1889-1900

Gertrude Robinson, age 22 - **Bridgeville Elementary School**

1900-1901

Gertrude Robinson and Bertha Robinson[17]

1902

Bertha Robinson, age 22

1903

Florence Knowles (Robinson)

1904

Florence Knowles (Robinson) (also taught at Showers Pass during in 1904)

1905

Florence Knowles (Robinson)

1906

Edna Swortzell

1907

Edna Swortzell

1908

Maude Hawks

1909

Rolla Bryant

1909-1910

Clara McCreery

1910-1911

Clara McCreery

1911-1912

1908 Teacher Maude Hawks with her class, Ed Wilkinson standing next to her in a hat.

1912-1913
Marian Albee
1913-1914
Jerrie Campton
1914-1915
Jerrie Campton
1916-1917
Aida Gerkey
George Underwood, County Superintendent of Schools
1917-1918
1918-1919
Lily Zimmerman
1919-1920
Easter Anita Cox[18]
1920-1921
Easter Anita Cox
1920-1921
Caltha Robinson, age 53 (taught at Buck Mt. School prior to Bridgeville)
1921-1922
Caltha Robinson, age 54[19]
1922-1923
Caltha Robinson, age 55
1923-1924
Caltha Robinson, age 56

A slightly different angle of Bridgeville School Building.

1924-1925
 Caltha Robinson, age 57
1925-1926
 Caltha Robinson, age 58
1926-1927
 Anita Easter (Cox) Mitchell, teacher
 W. E. Freenaty, Rural Supervisor
  The eighth grade graduates in 1927 were: Ada G. Campbell age 15, absent 4 days, and Victor G. Weisel age 14, absent 8 days. Last day of school: June 3, 1927.[20]
1927-1928
1928-1929
 Amelia G. Alward
 Grace C. Snodgrass
  There was one eighth grade graduate in 1929: Mildred Anna Burns age 13, absent 2 days. Last day of school: May 24, 1929.[21]
1929-1930
 Amelia G. Alward
 Grace C. Snodgrass
 W. E. Freenaty, Rural Supervisor
  The eighth grade graduates in 1930 were: Thomas Monroe Burns age 15, absent 1 day; Laura June Cox age 12, no absences; Eva Maxine Ceslie age 16, George Winfred Normile age 12, no absences; and Mary "Eleanor" Robinson age 12 no absences. Last day of school: May 29, 1930.[22]

1930-1931

Grace C. Snodgrass

The boys used their little pocket knives in a circle to play their game of Mumble Peg.[23] Audrey Campbell remembers that Miss Snodgrass came from a ranch in Petrolia and boarded at the hotel during the week. Miss Snodgrass taught the class about birdwatching.

1931-1932

Grace C. Snodgrass

The eighth grade graduates in 1932 were: Lester Barton Brinkman age 13, 3 days absent; Jennie Mae Burns age 14, no absences; Constance L. Cameron age 13, absent 1 day; and Audrey Mae Campbell age 13, absent 2 days. Last day of school: May 27, 1932.[24]

I remember that Miss Snodgrass would take a girl from class home with her to Petrolia for a special weekend treat. She only took girls, taking each girl only once, even though Miss Snodgrass had some students for more than one year.

—Audrey Campbell.[25]

Left: Graduating class of 1930 courtesy of William May. Miss Snodgrass on far left. Second from left is Eleanor Robinson (May) next to Winifred Normile. On the far right is Laura Cox (Pawlus) and the tall boy is Tom Burns. Right: Pictured to the right is Audrey Campbell circa 1938 (obviously not in first grade any longer!) Audrey Campbell lived on the William Drinkwater ranch (her mom's brother's ranch) when she went to Bridgeville School. Mrs. Alward was her teacher and she boarded at the hotel in town. Mrs. Alward taught Audrey to play the piano so she could play the song, "Good Morning to You" each day. On the playground they played Red Line and Kick the Bucket. Audrey remembers another student, Eleanor Robinson used to ride her horse to school.[26] Photo courtesy of Audrey Campbell.

1932-1933

Grace C. Snodgrass

At recess we had sticks we'd throw in the ground and flip it and wherever it lands is where you have to start out for the next round.

—Albert Hunt

1933-1934

Evelyn Shuster (Worthen)

L. E. Cuddeback,[27] Rural Supervisor

Ms. Shuster recorded that on Monday, August 13, 1933 it was 91 degrees at Bridgeville School, 102 degrees at the store, and 110 degrees in Chinatown. On hot days like this just before the boys entered the room they would douse their heads under the outside faucet, then flip their hair back before coming into the classroom.[28] The eighth grade graduates in 1934 were: Laura Lorene Burns age 15 and Anita Evangeline Weisel age 14. Last day of school: June 1, 1934.[29]

At Bridgeville School we had no electricity, no running water (except for the outside faucet by the building), and no modern rest rooms. There was no playground equipment, no school buses, and no mobile library. And of course, only one teacher for all eight grades in one room.

—Evelyn Shuster (Worthen)[30]

1934-1935

Evelyn Shuster (Worthen)

Cleaning out old files of student transfer papers, Mr. Mike Mullan in 2012 noted that many of those entering Bridgeville School during the 1930s were transferring from schools in Oklahoma, probably due to the Dust Bowl.[31] The eighth grade graduates in 1935 were: Arthur Dec Cottrell age 14, Frances Janet Griesbach age 13, James Greenwell Kinyon age 13, Dorothy June Smith age 14, and Wilda Elaine Smith age 13. Last day of school: June 11, 1936.[32]

1935-1936

Evelyn Shuster (Worthen)

Sometimes it snowed in the winter and the school was closed for much of the cold season. At one point Miss Shuster had five students named James in her class. A mother of a fifth grader, Lucile, asked if Miss Shuster ever spanked her. "Oh no," replied Lucile, "but when we are naughty, she looks so sad, we just have to be good." [33]

One day Miss Shuster was eating lunch by the Van Duzen River with the children. After lunch they returned to class and she began her lesson. She was surprised when numerous frogs started hopping around the floor. The children had brought them back in their pockets.[34] Miss Shuster stayed with the Cox family.

1936-1937
   Evelyn Shuster (Worthen)
   Margaret Jane Cotter
      There was one eighth grade graduates in 1937: James Edward
   Murray age 15. James Murray is the person that the VFW Hall in
   Pepperwood Falls was named after. Last day of school: May 28,
   1937.[35]

7th Grade May 24 1935

Seventh grade class in **1935**. From left to right: James Kinyon, Dee Cantrell, Alvirda
Murray, Willa Smith, Frances Griesbach and Dorothy Smith.

Last day of school May 28th 1935

Students on the last day of school, May 1935.

Picture courtesy of Humboldt County Historical Society. The eighth grade graduates of 1941. Third from left: Malcom "Make" Mead. Far right: Velda Wilkinson.

1937-1938
Margaret Jane Cotter
P. F. Woodcock, Rural Supervisor[36]
This is the first year that graduation paperwork refers to Bridgeville School District instead of Bridgeville School. The eighth grade graduates in 1938 were: Alice Lucille Leonard, age 13, Zolle Belle Mead, age 15, and Rolland Ellis Smith, age 14, graduating eighth graders on May 24, 1938.[37]

1938-1939
Margaret Jane Cotter
P. F. Woodcock, Rural Supervisor

1939-1941
Mrs. Lois Watkins

1941-1942
Mrs. Arline Delp[38]

1942-1943
Mrs. Adele Chaffey

1942

1943-1944
Mrs. Rita Hopper

1944-1945
Eve M. Beekman

1945-1946

Mrs. Irma E. Hellard

The "Old Gym" was built using lumber donated by a local mill and local residents provided the labor. Bridgeville residents built the gym in 1951. Outwardly, at least, it's a sturdy building with 2 by 12 inch planks on the floor and equally impressive beams in the ceiling. You couldn't pull this building over with a caterpillar tractor. But because it wasn't created with an official State Architect, the state of California is requiring us to take it down due to worries about earthquakes.

—Lola Cathey, 1985

1946-1947

Mrs. Verna C. Fowler (Crabtree), teacher[39]

The outhouse was one building but, there were separate stalls for boys and girls. The children were forbidden to play near the fat round propane tank on the school grounds. But, if Mrs. Fowler went into the classroom and left the children outside, they loved to get on it and play horsey. In those days if students misbehaved they would get smacked. Naughty children would go in class and be whacked on the buttocks two or three times in front of the whole class. That didn't really hurt, but the public humiliation of being spanked in front of the whole class meant that being disobedient was public knowledge, parents would find out and the real punishment would be at home.

—Jessie Wheeler

Bridgeville 8th grade class, from left to right with teacher Ms. Arline Delp: Majorie Shears, Louise Davis, Verna Mae Wilson, Arline Delp, Albert Hunt and May Davis standing in front of the porch of the original Bridgeville School. Photo courtesy of Humboldt Historical Society.

Bridgeville School bell tower circa 1949.

Bridgeville School 1949.

When we weren't in school, Dean Williams, Butch Green and I used to run around together shooting guns and riding bikes. We used to zoom past the store and hope no one would come out because we didn't have any brakes.

—Jay Card

1947-1948
Mrs. Verna C. Fowler (Crabtree), teacher
1948-1949
Mrs. Verna C. Fowler (Crabtree), teacher
P.T.A. President: Laura J. Pawlus
Enrollment: 61.[40]
This is the year that the P.T.A. is established. Folk Dancing is coming back in a big way to Humboldt County Schools.[41]
1949-1950
James S. Woodcock, principal
Mrs. Verna C. Fowler (Crabtree),[42] teacher
P.T.A. President: Wanda Sturm
Enrollment: 122.[43]
"Trustees and parents of Bridgeville Elementary School District cooperated again this summer for the third year in succession to add another fine classroom to their building. In addition to the

old building, Bridgeville now boasts three modern classrooms through the cooperative efforts of the trustees and parents."[44]

1950-1951

Mrs. Verna C. Fowler (Crabtree), principal
Robert Erwin[45]
Effy Rowley
Eva C. Stahl, 1-2[46]
P.T.A. President: Eufalla (Eufaulla) Bentley

According to some students Mrs. Stahl looked like a storybook witch with long dark hair, black dresses, and sturdy shoes. There was one little girl in the classroom who peed her pants. All the students had to go outside and stand in a line waiting for the little girl to clean it up. Then the little girl had to stand in a corner after she was publicly paddled. Mrs. Stahl paddled a lot, always in front of all the other children. Mrs. Stahl was overbearing with a loud voice and she would get right into a child's face, some of the kids were scared.[47]

Walt Mendenhall was the delivery guy who was a life line for Bridgeville School for 47 years. If you needed a ride into town he could give you a ride. Vanta Schuetzle said that her niece would ride into Fortuna with Walt, do shopping, spend a night or two and then ride back out with him.[48] Jessie Wheeler said her mom sometimes had her ride to town with Walt to Eureka in both grammar school and high school.

1951-1952

Don K. Williams, principal and 7-8 teacher[49]
Miss Virginia Lee Owen, 5-6

Gym built in 1951.

Jim Holt (right) and Dean Williams (left). Photo Courtesy of William C. May.

Miss Effy Rowley, 3-4
Mrs. Eva C. Stahl, 1-2[50]
P.T.A. President: Bernice Barkdull
Last day of school: June 17, 1952.
1952-1953
Don K. Williams, principal and 7-8 teacher
Donald R. Owen, 5-6
Virginia Lee Owen, 3-4
Mrs. Eva C. Stahl, 1-2
P.T.A. President: Irma Sturm
There were 17 eighth grade graduates this year ranging in age from 12 to 15 years old. Graduation was June 11, 1953.
The gym, as seen on the previous page, was there when I started school in 1953-54. But it was built only a couple years prior. The old school building that is in previous photos (as seen on page 17) connected to the gym in a "T" shape with the bell rope in the short hall between the two. The old building was the second grade classroom back in that time. The stage is on the right and raised right where you notice the siding change from grey to white. Under the stage there was an exterior door, visible in the photo (top of it appears over the fence), leading to the janitor's room where he kept supplies etc. The little window up high on the right was for stage ventilation. The two boys in the photo above are Jim Holt on the right and Dean Williams on the left. I don't know what happened to Dean but Jim became a CPA (like me) and is retired now living in the city of Paradise. He told me that his house was the only one on his block saved in the Paradise fire because the fire dept used it as a staging area.
—William C. May

Humboldt Land Title Company

215-217 6 STREET · EUREKA, CALIFORNIA · TELEPHONE MI 3-0637

AFFILIATED WITH

H. E. ARNOT, President

Land Title Insurance Company

October 21, 1954

Mr. George Cox
Bridgeville, California

Dear Mr. Cox:

The following is the legal description of the property
of the school site as per your request of today.

BEGINNING at the corner of Sections 11, 12, 13 and 14 in
Township 1 North of Range 3 East Humboldt Base and Meridian
and running thence North 20 degrees West 154 links, thence
South 247 links, thence West 274 links to the place of
beginning, containing six-tenths of an acre.

The description was taken from Deed executed by Edmund B.
Barnum and wife in favor of Trustees of Bridgeport School
District, recorded 12/9/1885.

If we can be of any further service to you please let us
hear from you.

Yours very truly,

Juanita O'Quinn
Escrow Officer

Letter courtesy of Jessie Wheeler.

There were four classrooms—the three old classrooms (as seen on page 23) that later burned down and the one behind the gym (as seen on page 18). There were two grades in each classroom, there wasn't a kindergarten.

—Mary Elizabeth Barnwell O'Connell

1953-1954

Mrs. Anita K. Mitchell, principal and 5-6
Joseph L. Brand, 7-8
Mrs. Lovesta D. Davis,[51] 3-4
Mrs. Eva C. Stahl, 1-2
P.T.A. President: Corbeny Moss

There were 18 eighth grade graduates this year ranging in age from 13 to 15 years old. Graduation was June 17, 1954. In 1954 the property of the current Bridgeville School (2025) was annexed from George H. Cox and Jessie H. Cox.

Mr. McWilliams with his eighth grade class.

1954-1955

Mrs. Anita K. Mitchell, principal and 6-7
L. R. McWilliams, 8 (Bob to his friends)
Mrs. Lovesta D. Davis, 4-5
Mrs. Leila E. Brandt,[52] 2-3
Mrs. Eva C. Stahl, 1
Mrs. Dorothy Arnold, part time music teacher
P.T.A. President: Mildred Voight

The eighth grade class of Bridgeville Elementary and their teacher, Bob McWilliams (a first year teacher), are learning about American Indians on a field trip to Eureka High School Museum seen above.

Old timers in the area who remembered the Wailaki Indians were invited to speak to the class. Tape recordings were made of the stories told by Everett Kay, Henry Cox, Ed Burns and William Barnwell. Above Mr. McWilliams is seen with his eighth grade class and Everett Kay.

—Bulletin Board, March 1955

Students remember Mrs. Brandt as being kind, soft spoken, and grandmotherly. She encouraged children to read by setting goals for reading so many books a week. I love to read to this day and I believe that Mrs. Brandt started me on the path of becoming a lifelong reader. Mrs. Brandt lived on Chalk Mountain Ranch. Sometimes I rode with her down to school and sometimes Mrs. Brandt rode the school bus.[53]

—Mary Elizabeth Barnwell O'Connell

Mrs. Brandt's second and third grade class from 1955 from left to right back row: Virginia May Rawlins, Nona Barkdull, Bonnie Johnson, Linda Murphy, Sue Larkins, Kathy Taylor, Jean Jorenson, Joyce Jenkins, Kathleen Hawkins, Georgia Cox, Georgia Mulliner, Patsy McCall, Ellen Crane, Zelma Howell and Shawn Morton. Second row: Jimmie Dan Cook, Gary Heimsoth, Mike Fraser, George Howell, Reed Charleton, Jack Phillips, Jimmy Holt, William May[54] and Robert Burliss. Front row: Kenny Church, Scotty McCall and Russel Hayes.

Mrs. Mitchell, pictured here, was the principal of Bridgeville School from 1953-1956. She also taught at Bridgeville in the 1920s and Buck Mountain in 1952. Photo courtesy of William C. May.

There were 13 eighth grade graduates this year ranging in age from 12 to 15 years old. Graduation was June 10, 1955.

1955-1956
Mrs. Anita K. Mitchell, principal and 5-6
Claude R. Parrish Jr., 7-8
Lenox R. McWilliams,[55] 3-4
Mrs. Leila E. Brandt, 1-2
Mrs. Dorothy Arnold, part time music teacher
P.T.A. President: James Coffer

1955 is the year that Bridgeville School first had electricity! There were 12 eighth grade graduates this year ranging in age from 13 to 16 years old. Graduation was June 8, 1956.

Mr. McWilliams lived in the house across the street from the school in Bridgeville. There was a time when they used to vote in the Quonset hut by there. After the Dust Bowl a lot of people were looking for work in Bridgeville and some of the timber workers had kids that had missed some schooling so a lot of the 8th graders were 15 or 16 years old.

Bridgeville School teacher Claude Parrish. He taught at Bridgeville School from 1955-1958. Photo courtesy of Jessie Wheeler.

William H. Barnwell Jr. was on the school board. He and others thought that they needed a big man to assist the school faculty handling the big boys, like the Adams boys who were physically big kids. They thought McWilliams could handle big kids and tough situations because he was previously a football player. During his job interview for the position someone asked him what he majored in during college.

Mr. Parrish with a parent Gloria Barnwell. Photo taken by and courtesy of William C. May.

"I majored in anatomy by braille on Fickle Hill Road," was the reply.

—Less Barnwell[56]

The year it flooded we just rolled our jeans up and ran across the creek, then we'd take our jeans off and go to school.

—Patsy Richardson

1956-1957

L. R. McWilliams, principal and 6-8
Claude R. Parrish Jr., 4-5
Ella Frances Gay, 2-3
Mrs. Leila E. Brandt, 1-2
Mrs. Dorothy Arnold, part time music teacher
P.T.A. President: Harry Toole

There were 12 eighth grade graduates this year ranging in age from 13 to 15 years old. Graduation was June 6, 1957.

Photo Courtesy of William C. May.

William and Mary Elizabeth on the playground. Photo Courtesy of William C. May.

Mrs. Brandt used to live within walking distance of the school. Mr. Brandt used to be gone a lot traveling all over the world. One time he came back and came to the classroom and told all the students about Alaska where he had just been.

—Rodney Jones

1957-1958

John A. Grisham, principal and 7-8
Claude R. Parrish Jr., 5-6
Mrs. Hazel F. Klemp, 3-4
Mrs. Leila E. Brandt, 1-2
James E. Westman
P.T.A. President: Frank Quadro (ranger at CDF)

There were 7 eighth grade graduates this year ranging in age from 13 to 14 years old. Graduation was June 5, 1958.

There were a lot of kids and the bus went two different ways. So those of us that went on the second run had after school recess. I was outside in orthopedic correction shoes stomping in mud puddles and someone caught a different student doing it and she had to sit in the classroom and was big trouble.

—Les Barnwell

Graduating class of 1958 [57] Wilma Mccall, Shirley Watson Ingram, Juanita Mullenex, Jessie Still, Bonnie Crabb, Dorene Watkins, Verna Ferguson, the other girls were Buck Mountain School graduates in town for the joint graduation ceremony. courtesy of William C. May.

1958 Easter Egg Hunt at Bar W. From left to right: 1. Ellen, 2. Christine Barkdull, 3.Patty Finnegan, 4. Virginia Rawlins, 5. Linda Murphy, 6. Nona Barkdull, 7. Cathy Taylor, 8. Leslie Hutton 9. Sue Larkins 10. Judy Ramsey 11. Kenny Larkins 12. Billy May 13. Mike Fraser 14. Jimmie Dan Cook 15. Dean Williams 16. Stephen Toole 17. Jim Holt 18. Mrs. Finnegan 19. Mrs. Anna Williams 20. Mr. and Mrs. Claude Barkdul 21. Mr. Parrish and Jay Dean.

Bridgeville Elementary 1958-1959 fifth and sixth grades.

1958-1959

> Clark Breeze, principal and 7-8
> Mrs. Jean Breeze, 3-4
> Mrs. Leila E. Brandt, 1-2
> Don Carter, 5-6
> Edward Solenberger, music teacher
> Gordon Crane, bus driver
> P.T.A. President: Edith Huberd (Mrs. Larry Huberd)
> Rodney Jones went to Bridgeville School in first and second grades and his teacher was Ms. Brandt. He remembers many of his friends there: Leslie Barnwell, Neil Barnwell, Bobby Sullivan, Debbie Hunt, Marsha Lytell and Mike Hime. The bus driver's name was Gordon Crane and he also did a lot of custodial work around the school. When Rodney attended there were only four classrooms and one of them was attached to the back of gymnasium. [58]

1959-1960

> Clark Breeze, principal and 7-8
> Mrs. Jean Breeze, 1-2
> Mrs. Bonnie Carter, 3-4
> Don Carter, 5-6
> Gordon Crane, bus driver
> P.T.A. President: Claude Barkdull

Photo is circa 1959. From left to right an unknown student, Mr. Breeze, Mrs. Breeze and Don Carter. Photo courtesy of William C. May.

Photo circa 1959 from left to right possibly Mr. Brandt, Mrs. Brandt and some unknown students, possibly Leslie Hutton in the white dress. Photo courtesy of William C. May.

1960-1961

Clark Breeze, principal and 7-8
Mrs. Jean Breeze, 1-2
Mrs. Bonnie Carter, 3-4
Don Carter, 5-6
Gordon Crane, bus driver
P.T.A. President: Don Carter

Don Carter lived on Sturm Ranch and Mrs. Bonnie Carter was beautiful. They drove one of the first Volvos in the area. The school bus would occasionally pick her up.

—Les Barnwell

Don Carter was a great teacher.

—Rita Baker

Mr. Clark Breeze made education fun.

—Patsy Richardson

1960 Television comes to Bridgeville with a double wire on trees for an antenna, but you had to go two miles up the hill to get reception. There was only one channel, KIEM Channel 3. Television was live then and it came on at noontime and went off at midnight.

—Jessie Wheeler

There was strict discipline at Bridgeville School. My first grade teacher had a yard stick and if you were out of line she used it. Mr. Crane had a two handled paddle. He was a really nice guy, but if you had it coming he would give you swats, like for leaning against the cyclone fence and then we didn't do it anymore.

—Richard Church

1961-1962
Mary Brandenburg, principal and 4-6
Robert E. Baird, 7-8
Ethel M. Kahne, 1-3
Keith Chaffey, speech therapist
Gordon Crane, bus driver
P.T.A. President: William Barnwell III

Gordon Crane was a beloved bus driver and custodian at Bridgeville School. He smoked on the school bus, with his window open. Gordon lived on the Chalk Mountain Ranch and worked sheep and cattle on the ranch. He had his own horse and stock dogs. Mr. Crane drove the school bus. He worked 6 days a week at the

1961 photo of Mr. and Mrs. Breeze. Photo courtesy of William C. May.

school. He would make school bus runs in the mornings by keeping the school bus at his house. From his house he would drive to Alderpoint, Burr Creek, then drive to Highway 36 to Fords Flat, and drive back go to Bridgeville School, dropping off the kids. Then he would make the Swains Flat run. Sometimes he would work all day at school, do the bus run and then in the afternoon he would park the bus at his home and take his pickup back to school for custodial chores.

Everything was pristine. He mowed the Baseball diamond all the time, as it was in constant use. One day some boy(s) sneaked into the girls restroom and wrote a bad word(s) on the mirror with lipstick. It was a big deal. They were all questioned individually about it. It was quite a ruckus.

—Mary Elizabeth Barnwell O'Connell

Gordan Crane drove the bus all eight years I went to Bridgeville School.

—Dan Phillips

Left is Gordon Crane after whom the "new gym" was named circa 1985. Right: Janice Crane with Gordon. Janice was the Bridgeville School Secretary, first as a volunteer, than later as a paid position for many years. She was a stickler for details. Photos courtesy of George Brightman.

Mrs. Brandenburg was the principal when I was in Mr. Baird's class. It was the early 60s, so girls and women were still not wearing pants on a regular basis. Previously the kids, including girls, wore shorts to school in the warmer months. But, when Mrs. Brandenburg came to Bridgeville School all the girls had to wear dresses, so we wore shorts under our dresses. We loved the monkey bars, the high jump and baseball so that is what we played during recess. Our skirts were flying up all the time, luckily we were wearing shorts underneath!

—Mary Elizabeth Barnwell O'Connell

1962-1963

Mary Brandenburg (Jardin), principal and 4-6
Robert E. Baird, 7-8
Ethel M. Kahne, 1-3
Keith Chaffey, speech therapist
Janice Crane, volunteer secretary
Gordon Crane, bus driver and custodian
P.T.A. President: Albert Hunt

My brother Neil Barnwell and I always noticed that the Sequoia Gas tank had a sign that instructed, "no smoking within 50 feet." But, being kids, we didn't really think about it the same way an adult would. When we noticed that the grass had grown up around the gas tank; we knew what a fire hazard tall grass could be. So, we lit the grass to burn it down before there was a problem. Boy did we get in trouble. That was the only time that Gordon Crane was known to paddled students.

—Les Barnwell

Mr. Baird lined the whole class up on the new wire fence and told us to stay off the bank. He used the paddle to reinforce behavior. My Dad went and talked to him and I never got spanked.

—Jay Card

When I started teaching at Bridgeville, Gordon Crane looked me up and down and said, "you look like city folk. Don't worry, I'll teach you to be country folk."

—Mike Grady

On Arbor Day, April 10, 1962 the students in all three classrooms wrote their names on lined manuscript paper and each teacher placed the sheet of paper in a mason jar. Gordon Crane, our custodian, sealed the jar and placed it in a hole he had dug earlier in preparation for a sycamore tree to be planted at the same spot. A program of songs and poems and a brief history of Arbor

Bridgeville School circa 1964. We can see the "old bus barn" is just left of center. The wood fence of the early 1960's is gone. Most of that playground equipment will be there for another 25 years. The access to the school was still down the CDF road, seen in the lower right hand corner and through what is now called "the old gate." Photo courtesy of William C. May.

Day was presented. The sycamore tree was planted in the hole. We all watched as Mr. Crane filled the hole with soil.

—Mary Brandenburg (Jardin)

They had just plowed the playground area and we were told to stay off the dirt banks. Every boy in school got a good swat.

—Ken McCall

1963-1964

Mary Brandenburg (Jardin), principal and 4-6
Robert E. Baird, 6-8
Ethel M. Kahne, 1-3
Keith Chaffey, speech therapist
P.T.A. lists Meriam G. Boyd as a teacher[59]
Janice Crane, volunteer secretary
Gordon Crane, bus driver and custodian
P.T.A. President: Wayne Malm and Betty Hunt

1964-1965

Mary Brandenburg (Jardin), principal and 1-2
Elbert B. Burdick, 6-8
Mrs. Margery P. Murray, 3-5 and music teacher
Keith Chaffey, speech therapist
Janice Crane, secretary
Gordon Crane, bus driver and custodian
P.T.A. President: Gloria Barnwell
Eighth graders learned square dancing, the Bossa Nova, and the Salty Dog Rag at a feeder school event hosted by Fortuna High.

The washed out access road going into the Bridgeville Fire Station in December 1964. The view is to the east towards the station.

1964 was the year of the Christmas holiday flood. One rancher reported twelve inches of rain in a 24 hour period. The flood lasted longer than the Christmas break and people were isolated in Bridgeville for about four weeks. The kids attending high school in town, of which I was one, didn't go. Then a temorary road to west Fortuna was cleared.

—Rex Fisher[60]

Bridgeville School has a large trampoline. I hope to add archery and tennis to our exercise program and game based P.E.
—Elbert Burdick[61]

The primary purpose of our Bridgeville P.E. program is to broaden the range of children's experiences in taking turns, having fun, being good sports, and the development of muscles, coordination, rhythm, and confidence.
—Mary Brandenburg (Jardin)[62]

Mr. Burdick tried to break up a fight between Mike Crawford and me. We ended up breaking the railing on the porch and in the end Mike got suspended.
—Les Barnwell

1965-1966
Elbert B. Burdick, principal and 6-8
Mrs. Mary Brandenburg (Jardin), 1-2
Daniel Nobel, 3-5
Keith Chaffey, speech therapist
DuWayne Olds, music teacher
Janice Crane, secretary

Gordon Crane, bus driver and custodian

P.T.A. President: James Olsen

A program demonstrating training and development of talent in music, drama, and speech was presented to an appreciative audience at the Bridgeville P.T.A. meeting in April. Under the direction of Mr. DuWayne Olds and Mrs. Mary Brandenburg, the entire student body participated in a delightful concert.

Primary grades presented an exciting Operetta "The Three Billy Goats' Gruff." Cast: Steven Burdick-Little Billy Goat, Jimmy Bramlette-Big Billy Goat, and Steven Olsen-Great Billy Goat. The Chorus and Trolls were played by: Raymond Parkhurst, Russell Burdick, Ricky Iverson, Dan Phillips, Crystal Barnwell, Jimmy Dawson, Owen Anderson and Susan Iverson.

Orinda Barnwell played the violin, Terri Hunt played the Bells, Nancy Porter played the Autoharp. Crystal Barnwell, Nancy Porter, and Russell Burdick also played the piano. The climax of the evening was a rousing Hootenanny with audience participation.

—*Bulletin Board*, June 1966

Creativity is practical, and Bridgeville students show it is practical to be creative. Not only have students formed a singing group after learning the E-minor chord on the guitar from Mrs. Mabel Anderson of the Humboldt County, but they are inventors too. David Card, the leader of The Impossibles, has fashioned an improved shoe holder for shoe shiners. Phillip Porter has devel-

Mr. Elbert B. Burdick
Principal

Bridgeville Elementary School
Bridgeville, California
1965 - 66

Mr. Noble
Teacher - Third-Fourth-Fifth Grade

Mr. Noble pictured with his class circa 1965.

The Bridgeville School folk singing group The Impossibles is led by David Card in front and supported by (from left to right in the back row) Henry Barnwell, Dennis Ford and Ronald Dawson.

oped a method whereby he can guarantee his matches won't burn your fingers. Dennis Ford, after wrestling with the problem of sandling wood scupture has now produced a simple sanding device every student can make.

—Larry Kaiser[63]

We enjoyed a program of Christmas music played for us by the Rohnerville Mini Band. We do not have a school sponsored band experience for students and this is a real treat.

—John Leasure, principal

1966-1967
Elbert B. Burdick, principal and 6-8
Richard Shaner, 3-5
Mary Burdick, 1-2
Keith Chaffey, part time speech therapist
DuWayne Olds, part time music teacher
Janice Crane, secretary
Gordon Crane, bus driver and custodian
P.T.A. President: Gloria Barnwell

1967-1968
Larry Kaiser, principal and 6-8
John R. Leasure Jr., 3-5
Mrs. Kaiser, K-2

(P.T.A. records say Mrs. Mary White Arneson)
Keith Chaffey, part time speech therapist
Mrs. Mirtha Comas, Spanish teacher
Janice Crane, secretary
Gordon Crane, bus driver and custodian
P.T.A. President: Roberta Iverson
First year of Bridgeville School offering kindergarten.

The students all began as privates or minutemen in either the British or American Army and from there rose to the rank of staff sergeant in the course of one week. Every student earned at least one stripe and wore it. Larry Kaiser made the game called *Armageddon* as a motivational tool.

The students move fleets, armies, wagon trains, and artillery over 2,000 odd squares superimposed over a huge world map. They earn a move or can purchase a fighting unit by completing assignments.

—*Bulletin Board* [64]

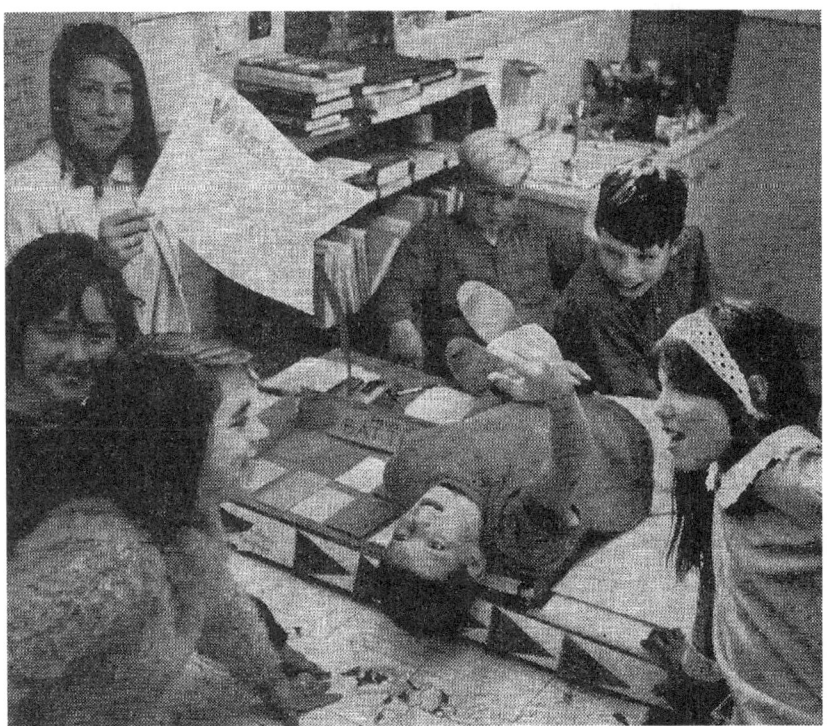

Bridgeville School students celebrate a Vocabulary Victory ending a gruelling Naval battle in their seventh and eighth grade class game *Armageddon*. Left to right they are: Elizabeth Mulvihill, Cathy Seidell, Joyce Baker, Asa Wall, Steve and Phillip Porter and Dawn Shuping, while Henry Barnwell provides corpus de Victoria.

Gordon Crane, Bridgeville School bus driver and Ward Bartlett at Pawlus home in Bridgeville, 1968. Photo courtesy of Jessie Wheeler.

Bridgeville School qualified for the so-called culturally disadvantaged entitlements of the ESEA Title I project and with the money, went in search of music, art and urban culture.

—*Bulletin Board* [65]

1968-1969

Larry Kaiser, principal and 6-8
John R. Leasure Jr., 3-5
Mrs. Margaret (Peggy) Rice, K-2 (at right)
Keith Chaffey, part time speech therapist
Mrs. Mirtha Comas, Spanish teacher
Janice Crane, secretary
Gordon Crane, bus driver and custodian

The school's average daily attendance (ADA) during the 1968-69 school year was 55.

1969-1970

Mrs. Ward, principal and 3-5
Stewart Fauerback & Leasure, 6-8
Mrs. Margaret (Peggy) Rice, K-2
Keith Chaffey, part time speech therapist
Mrs. Mirtha Comas, Spanish teacher
Janice Crane, secretary
Gordon Crane, bus driver and custodian

1970-1971

Mr. John Leasure, principal and 6-8
Mrs. Margaret (Peggy) Rice, K-2
Ms. Bonnie Williams, 3-5
Keith Chaffey, part time speech therapist
Mrs. Mirtha Comas, Spanish teacher

A 1971 music program inside the gym with students sitting or laying on grey wrestling mats that were still there in 1986. The visiting students from Rohnerville are playing up on the stage: Keith Demello, Matthew Sharkey and Ken Rasmussen on trumpets; Ron Metcaf on trombone, Steven Roberts on baritone saxaphone and Jim Bramlett on drums.[66]

1971-1972
Mr. John Leasure, principal and 6-8
Mrs. Margaret (Peggy) Rice, K-2
Lola Cathey, 3-5
Keith Chaffey, part time speech therapist
Janice Crane, secretary
Gordon Crane, custodian
Enrollment: 31

Peggy Rice was an energetic and dedicated teacher/educator with grades K, 1 and 2. I assisted her as an aide in 1974-1975. Mrs. Rice was always accepting, loving and spot on that her students would have fun learning at a young age. Peggy handled all the details that came from the state each year, meaning new subject matter, rules, tests, etc. I loved working with Peggy Rice and she was always on time.

—Linda McClure

I remember us going to the Crane's home one evening while my stepfather, Larry Kaiser, was principal sometime between '66-69. I remember the Cranes brought out some board games that we played. That may have been in part because there wasn't any television reception.

—Dixie Lee Ducote

1972-1973
  Mrs. Margaret (Peggy) Rice, K-2
  Lola Cathey, 3-5 and principal
  Mr. John Leasure, 6-8
  Keith Chaffey, part time speech therapist

BRIDGEVILLE — Peggy Rice starts her 15th year at the school, teaching kindergarten and first grade, by re-decorating the room's bulletin board walls.

Peggy Rice pictured in the *Humboldt Beacon*, September 1, 1983.

  Third grade teacher, Lola Cathey's great, great, grandparents were Mary and John Brown; descendants of John Brown of Harper Ferry fame. His son, Salmon Brown owned the land next to Bridgeville School at one point. Brown Creek (which runs by the school) is named after them.[67]

  At some point the sycamore, under which the time capsule from 1962 was buried, had to be removed. Janice Crane asked the workers to keep an eye out for the mason jar that held the student's names. They found it, she framed them and hung them in her office.

1973-1974
  Mrs. Margaret (Peggy) Rice, K-2
  Lola Cathey, 3-5
  John R. Leasure, 6-8
  Keith Chaffey, part time speech therapist

1974-1975
  Mrs. Margaret (Peggy) Rice, K-2
  Lola Cathey, 3-5 and principal
  Mr. Davis, 6-8
  Keith Chaffey, part time speech therapist
  Linda McClure, primary aide

1975-1976
  Mrs. Margaret (Peggy) Rice, K-2
  Lola Cathey, 3-5 and principal
  Joe Brewer, 6-8
  Keith Chaffey, part time speech therapist

1976-1977

Mrs. Margaret (Peggy) Rice, K-2

Lola Cathey, 3-5 and principal

John Arriaga, 6-8

Nina Kayes, part time speech therapist

1977-1978

Mrs. Margaret (Peggy) Rice, K-2

Lola Cathey, 3-5 and principal

John Arriaga, 6-8

Nina Kayes, part time speech therapist

Dwight May saw a fire burning at Bridgeville School the morning of March 30, 1978. Mr. May called CDF fire captain Ernie Jarvis, who lived close to the school. Two-thirds of the Bridgeville Elementary School was destroyed by fire early Tuesday morning with an estimated loss of $100,000 for buildings and contents. Two classrooms and the school offices were lost, but the auditorium, gym and one classroom were saved.

—Times Standard

By the time Dwight May saw the fire the flames were coming out the windows and through the roof. Ernie Jarvis saved one of the rooms. He was working by himself—the closest CDF engine was 35 minutes away. Ernie was probably really hustling for 35 minutes.

—Wes Shamblin, CDF

The school burned down on Thursday and Lola Cathey called us and asked us to bring supplies out for the kids. On Friday there she was, having school on the playground. She didn't miss a beat.

—Helen from HCOE

We are doing just great. Desks, books and other materials destroyed in the fire have been temporarily replaced with supplies borrowed from other schools.

—Lola Cathey

A Fire in the Bridgeville School broke out on March 30, 1978. Two-thirds of the Bridgeville Elementary School was destroyed by fire early Tuesday morning with an estimated loss of $100,000 for buildings and contents. Two classrooms and the school offices were lost, but the auditorium-gym and one classroom were saved.

—Humboldt Beacon

The famed *Time Capsule* was burned and the glass melted. Janice Crane took the bits and put them in a cupboard. There were

40 students at Bridgeville School in 1978 according to the *Humboldt Beacon* or 54 students if you'd rather believe the *Times Standard*.

The great thing about this picture is that you can see the old bell tower, library (#2), and gym to the left, what would become the "old library" (#3) and teacher supply room on the right; and the new "temporary portable classrooms" in the middle which are still in use as of the time of this printing. Check out where the basketball hoop is.

What was used as the kindergarten or first grade room for decades is being installed, after the fire debris was removed, as part of the new "temporary portable classrooms." When school enrollment dropped after its height of 149 this room became a storage area or a place for small groups to meet. In 2022 it became a ceramics room. The old gym, built by local residents, can be seen at the right. It was condemned by Humboldt County Office of Education risk management, not because it was unstable but because state architects had not been used in the planning. (this was also the fate of the library seen on page viii.)

1978-1979
Mrs. Margaret (Peggy) Rice, K-2
Lola Cathey, 3-5 and teaching principal
Mike Grady, 6-8 and vice principal
Nina Kayes, part time speech therapist
    This was the first Year Mike Grady, Lola Cathey, and Peggy Rice worked together. They formed a core group of employees who worked at Bridgeville School for a minimum of 17 years providing an unprecedented stability. The Average Daily Attendance: (ADA) was 50.[68] By February 1979, there was a new three room school at Bridgeville. Fire insurance covered the cost.

1980-1981
Mrs. Margaret (Peggy) Rice, K-2
Lola Cathey, 3-5 and teaching principal/superintendent
Mike Grady, 6-8 and vice principal
Nina Kayes, part time speech therapist

1981-1982
Mrs. Margaret (Peggy) Rice, K-2
Lola Cathey, 3-5 and teaching principal/superintendent
Mike Grady, 6-8 and vice principal
Nina Kayes, part time speech therapist
    The gym serves as the cafeteria and auditorium, the stage doubles as a speech therapy section, the kitchen is also the library and pre-school room and the custodian's former workroom is also used as a classroom.

                              —Lola Cathey[69]

1982-1983
Mrs. Margaret (Peggy) Rice, K-2
Lola Cathey, 3-5 and teaching principal/superintendent
Mike Grady, 6-8 and vice principal
Nina Kayes, part time speech therapist
P.T.A. President Joann Duey

1983-1984
Lola Cathey, 4 and teaching principal/superintendent
Peggy Rice, K-1
Kathy Thatcher (Larson), 2-3
Keith Larson, 4-5
Mike Grady, 6-8
Nina Kayes, part time speech therapist
Geri Linari, special education teacher
P.T.A. President: Joann Duey
    I attended Bridgeville School from kindergarten through the eighth grade. I graduated in 1983. My teachers were Mrs. Rice (my favorite teacher ever), Mrs. Cathey and Mr. Grady. Part of the

school burned down when I was in (I think) the third grade. That is when we had to move into the gym. For a while, there was a funky curtain at half court to separate Mrs. Cathey's class from Mr. Grady's. Then they built a wall. The little kids were in the library/kitchen. We had to travel for all our basketball games because we didn't have a gym, which was kind of OK because the rafters of the building made it difficult to shoot from very far away anyway. (At the time, one of the end zones on our football field was also at the top of a steep hill.) We moved into the new building when I was in the fifth grade. It was very exciting to have all new stuff.

—Kristin Winbigler

Mr. Grady never gave up on a kid. He would stay until all hours of the night to have a student finish an assignment. He just kept saying, "You will stay here with me until you get this done." One time he stayed with John until 8:00 p.m. Mr. Grady suggested to John that he pay me for gas money since I had to pick him up after the bus run.

—Julie Stephens

I went to Bridgeville from kindergarten to 6th grade. I think it was 1985 when I left. Some of my favorite times were the movies in the gym on the reel to reel; I want to say it was *Blazing Saddles* or *The Apple Dumpling Gang* maybe both. Donkey basketball was a good one where the men had to wear boxing gloves and play basketball against women. I won a spelling bee and still to this day have the trophy. I remember the day Mrs. Jarvis got a new car (Volkswagen station wagon-UGLY). The whole school came out to see her new car. In the mini society I was a professional beggar and did pretty well until it got out of hand and they had to shut it down. We also had to stand up and recite all the states and

Mrs. Rice's 1983-1984 kindergarten and first grade class.

John Stephens and Mike Grady in 1985.

capitals. I still remember 90% of them today. I remember plant-ing the trees on the top of the hill that are now huge!! Looking back it was a great place to be from, I loved the school and hated it! Thank you Mrs. Rice, Mrs. Leroy (my first crush) Mr. Larson, Mrs. Thatcher, Mr. Grady and all the support that helped that little school play a big part in so many lives.

—Mike Dotson

In 1983 there were 80 students. The Average Daily Atten-dance: (ADA) was 77. The School Site Council consisted of Lola Cathey, Peggy Rice, Barbara Brightman, Joann Duey, Annette Church and Sandy Richards. They worked on providing a fine arts program.

In 1984 the back portion of the school (the library/study area) were still part of the one room schoolhouse on this site. In 1984 you could still see the place where the bell rope came through the ceiling in the anteroom, which was a storage area then. The six old windows were still there then, despite many renovations.

1984-1985
Lola Cathey, principal
Peggy Rice, K-1
Kathy Thatcher Larsen, 2-3
Virginia Howard Mullan, 5-6
Mike Grady, 6-8 and vice principal
Geri Linari, special education teacher
Nina Kayes, part time speech therapist
Enrollment: 96.[70]

1985-1986[71]
  Lola Cathey, principal
  Cindy Dibkey [Tuisku], K
  Peggy Rice, 1-2
  Linda Lienkaemper, 3-4
  Virginia Howard Mullan, 5-6
  Mike Grady, 7-8 and vice principal
  Geri Linari, special education teacher
  Nina Kayes, part time speech therapist
  P.T.A. President: Cindy Ritter
  Founders Day Honoree: Janice Crane

 I went to Bridgeville in the 8th grade, twice! Yes Mr. Grady held me back, lol. I'm very glad he did. I loved Mr. Grady! He made me like school for the first time! I always loved mini society. I think thats what it was called. I brought my makeup and nail polish and set up shop. There were six kids that graduated with me... Ezra, Brian, Kevin, Rosie, Brenda and myself. I moved to Fortuna and would sometimes ride with Mrs. Cathey to school. Sorry to bring this up, some of us would walk to the Bridgeville Store at lunch and buy a can of beer and guzzle it before returning to school. Yes, the store sold us beer. What rebels we were. Laurel Remington was my best friend. Kirk Lange was my boyfriend from another school. I was just too shy. Not too shy to buy beer though. I loved the dances! I think I remember dancing with Kevin Tomilla. I loved everyone who went to Bridgeville!!!

—Celia Marie Renner

Graduation 1986 outside by the old backstop. Left to right: Christy Jarvis, Robert Huston, Ben Johnson and Mike Grady.

I know I was in Kindergarten in 1985-86. I had Mrs. Tuisku. We were in the portable building down by the gym, kind of where the sea-train sheds are now.

—Brooke Johnston

1986-1987

Lola Cathey, principal
Cindy Dibkey Tuisku, K
Peggy Rice, 1
Linda Leinkaemper, 2-3
Virginia Howard Mullan, 5-6
Mike Grady, 7-8 and vice principal
Geri Linari, special education teacher
Nina Kayes, part time speech therapist
P.T.A. President: Kelly Remington
Founders Day Honorees: Rick and Chris Johnson

1987-1988

Lola Cathey, principal
Cindy Tuisku and Ms. Havard, K
Peggy Rice and Corinne Fearrien, 1-2
Betty Vogt, 2-3
Virginia Howard Mullan, 5-6
Mike Grady, 7-8 and vice principal
Geri Linari, special education teacher
Nina Kayes, part time speech therapist
P.T.A. President: Pam Walker
Founders Day Honoree: Lola Cathey

1988 Graduation Ms. Lola Cathey, Tim Smith, Debbie Bowman and Leslie McGill

Throughout the years many students and staff enjoyed the "end of the year picnic" at Pamplin Grove. There were also nature walks, volleyball, crafts, some years beading or Ms. Fearrien's bubbles, sometimes awards & report cards were handed out, there was sometimes swimming, and always a great lunch. CDF (now Cal Fire) have been generous with presentations as seen with Smokey and Ms. Fearrien's class.

Bridgeville School in 1989 when there was still the stage portion of the old gym (seen on the far left) and the old Bus Barn on the right before it was moved closer to Kneeland Road. The first office portable (where today's Bridgeville School Office is located) can be seen just behind and left of the bus barn. Only the room adjacent to the Gordon Crane Gym was built at that time. There was no breezeway in 1989.

1988-1989
Lola Cathey, principal
Alice Oliphant and Cindy Tuisku, K
Peggy Rice and Corinne Fearrien, 1
Kary Karges, 2-3
Betty Vogt, 3-4
Virginia Howard Mullan, 5-6
Mike Grady, 7-8 and vice principal
Geri Linari, special education teacher
Nina Kayes, speech therapist
P.T.A. President: Patty Hess
Founders Day Honorees: George Brightman and Cathey Jarvis

1989-1990
Mike Grady, principal
Cindy Tuiskku and Alice Oliphant, K
Peggy Rice and Corinne Fearrien, 1-2
Bernadette Regli-Church, 4-5
Chris Cooper, 5-6
Virginia Howard Mullan, 7-8 and vice principal
Geri Linari, special education teacher
Nina Kayes, part time speech therapist
P.T.A. President: Ms. Mullan
Founders Day Honoree: Mike Grady

Bridgeville School in 1990.

MIKE GRADY
Principal

BRIDGEVILLE SCHOOL
Bridgeville, California
1990-1991

MRS. MULLAN-Mr. COOPER
Grades 6-7-8

FRONT ROW: Jacob Scaife, Chano Cruz, Jeremy Buckner, Mike Brinson, Mike Asbury SECOND ROW: Daniel Bywater, Jessica Gatlin, Jenny Peterson, Sherry Jackson, Ruth Jackson, Addie Faustine, Tiffany Hunt, Jessica Wojcik, Shannon Dresen, Alice Hess THIRD ROW: Mr. Cooper-Teacher, Mr. Grady-Dist. Supt., Robyn Samuelson, Prairie Johnston, Leah Sheline, Monika Little, Yana Sweeney, Samantha Gray, Amber Simmons, Heidi Day, Honey Schmidt, Nichole Christensen, Joyce Church-Aide FOURTH ROW: John Buckner, Danny Foster, Nathan Middleton, Brent Bennett, Jacob Middleton, Matt Christensen, Mike McEnry, Cody Hess, Shawn Day, Mrs. Mullan-Teacher, Cathy Jarvis-Aide NOT PICTURED: Maria Mann-Gugne

Bridgeville sixth, seventh and eighth grades, class of 1990-91.

1990-1991

    Mike Grady, principal
    Cindy Tuisku and Kathy Wood, K-1
    Peggy Rice and Corinne Fearrien, 1-2
    Barry Blake, 3-4
    Bernadette Church, 4-5
    Chris Cooper and Virginia Howard Mullan, 6-8
    Geri Linari, special education teacher
    Nina Kayes, part time speech therapist
    Lew Johnson, music teacher
    Dottie Simmons, yearbook advisor

    Mrs. Rice's class held a Mother's Day Tea. Mr. Blake's class made candy for Valentine's Day to sell and it was delicious. Alice Hess, Leah Sheline and Tiffany Hunt created a cheer-leading squad complete with pom poms and uniforms. They went to the boys basketball games and competed in Scotia. The Math Team went to two events and Olympics of the Mind. Three students won first place at the County Science Fair in their division: Matthew Hunt, Tiffany Hunt and Samantha Gray.[72] The sixth and seventh grade participated in the first ever 24-Hour Relay at Albee Stadium in Eureka, sleeping on the field and running all night May 18-19.[73]

1991-1992

    Mike Grady, principal
    Peggy Rice and Corinne Fearrien, 1-2
    Barry Blake, 2-3

Bernadette Church, 4-5
Chris Cooper, 6-8
Virginia Howard Mullan, vice principal
Geri Linari, special education teacher
Nina Kayes, part time speech therapist
Nancy French, reading specialist*
Lew Johnson, music teacher

1991   BRIDGEVILLE SCHOOL   1992

MR. GRADY, SUPERINTENDENT-PRINCIPAL   STAFF
ROW 2: KATHY WOOD, VIRGINIA HOWARD-MULLAN, KATHLEEN SMITH, DANA JOHNSTON, MICHAEL GRADY, CHRISTOPHER COOPER,
MICHAEL CARROLL, BARRY BLAKE, JEANIE CARD, ANNETTE CHURCH *ROW 1:* LINDA GRIESBACH, JEANNE REID, DIANE PERKIN, DOUG
SNYDER, RINDY SAMUELSON, LORI SHELINE, NANCY FRENCH, MARY ANN BYWATER, MARYLIN GRADY, JOYCE CHURCH, BARBARA
BRIGHTMAN *ABSENT:* BERNADETTE CHURCH, CORINNE FEARRIEN, GERI LINARI, NINA KAYES, LEWIS JOHNSON, BETH ROSS

Bridgeville 1991-92 teachers.

Math Team from left to right: Ryan Samuelson, Samantha Gray, Tonde Razooly, Yana
Sweeney, Amber Simmons, Kyle Ritter, Brent Bennett, Leah Sheline and Alice Hess.

Varsity Volley Ball Team back row from left to right: Yana Sweeney, Shanon Bowman, Heidi Day and Samantha Gray. Front row: Honey Schmidt, Amber Simmons and Leah Sheline. The volleyball team won the Eel River Valley Schools Tournament and then went to the Coos Bay tournament winning 4th in their division.

    I was volunteering for the read-a-thon in Mr. Grady's room when my three year old, Dustin, turned off the surge protector to which the four computers in the room were connected. The junior high kids weren't thrilled, but Mr. Grady calmed them down and was sweet to Dustin. Mr. Grady even gave Dustin one of the jelly beans, he was famous for, to smooth his distress.[74]

                                   —Pam Walker

    In spring of 1992, after 21 years of service, beloved teacher Peggy Rice retires (hired in 1968). Mrs. Rice was well known for her excellent science and reading programs in the primary grades. Students also remember field trips and sleepovers at her ranch.

1992-1993

Mike Grady, principal
Barry Blake
Chris Cooper
Mike Carrol
Phyllis Taborski and Virginia Howard Mullan, 7-8
Craig Guptill, special education teacher
Nina Kayes, part time speech therapist
Lew Johnson, music teacher

Row 3: Serenity (Ren) Samuelson, Sara Shively, Shaman Wickham, Everson Corrigan, Monica Henson, Mike Loveless, Linden Wood and Jay Heflin. Row 2: Patrick Marshall, Gigi Heflin, Jericho Schmidt, Rebecca Corrigan and Ms. Mullan. Row 1: Ms. Samuelson, Mr. Johnston, Mr. Grady, Aaron Blendell, Mr. Guptill, J.R. Dunlap, Ms. Owen and Mr. Cooper. Absent: Shaun Wildman.

When Mike Grady was a teacher he used to make 40 cups of coffee each day in the teachers' workroom for any of the parents, volunteers or staff to enjoy. He loved coffee. After the Thanksgiving Feast there was coffee left over so I asked Julie Stephens what to do with it. We decided to can the coffee in a quart mason jar and put it in the cupboard with a label, "Save for Mr. Grady in case of emergency."[75]

—Pam Walker

1993-1994

Mike Grady, principal and 4-8
Kathy Wood, K
Nancy French, 1-2
Corinne Fearrien, 1-2
Barry Blake, 2-3
Chris Cooper, 4-8
Phyllis Taborski, 4-8
Virginia Howard Mullan, 4-8 and vice principal
Craig Guptill, special education teacher
Nina Kayes, part time speech therapist
Rachel Owen, substitute teacher

Above presentation of floor plan given by Florine Hilliard, Jolene Card, Jessica Brinson and Chris Hulslander. The shelves, stage, and design of the current Bridgeville School Library was created by students during the 1993-1994 school year. There was a class of 24 fourth through sixth grade students that met on Tuesdays and Wednesdays with Ms. Mullan for two trimesters. In the picture above you can see some of the culmination projects in which students proposed designs for the floor plan of the new library. Students used logic, measurement, spatial reasoning, perseverance and cooperation. Students studied perimeter, area. They used catalogs to find items and consulted with the librarian and administration about preferences and limitations. Two students joined the adult restructuring library planning committee. The class took a field trip to where the shelves were to be made and picked out the stain for the wood. Students' names are all written on the studs of the current library, hidden by drywall and paint. To the right construction begins on the new wing.

Ms. Taborski during graduation 1994.

Ms. Taborski's writing class created fabulous "Blazer News" Newsletters which were recognized by Louis Bucher, ED.D. the superintendent of schools who wrote, "I am quite impressed with the quality of your newsletter. It is outstanding!"

In science we learned about mollusks, we dissected oysters, named the parts and then BBQ ninety oysters for the students to taste. Our excellent cook, Pam Walker, co-coordinated an Egyptian feast that coincided with the 6th grade unit on Egypt and we coordinated a Hanukkah feast in December.

—Ms. Mullan[76]

Mike Grady's class read *Shabanu, The Cat that Wore Earrings, Indian in the Cupboard* and *Gullivers Travels.*[77]

Mr. Guptill carried Shree Morris and Cassie Williams on his back down the steep hill at Patrick's Point so they could, "run their toes in the sand."

Bridgeville becomes a special Senate Bill 1274 restructuring school receiving $24,600.00 in extra funds for each of the next five years from the state government.[78] Some of these funds help create the Community Center and pay for services.[79]

1994-1995

Mike Grady, principal transitions into Management Team
Kathy Wood, K-1
Corinne Fearrien, K-1
Barry Blake, 2-3
Rachel Owen, music teacher and independent study
Chris Cooper, 4-8
John Blakely, 4-8
Virginia Howard Mullan, 4-8, vice principal and yearbook
Nancy French, Miller Unruh reading teacher
Nina Kayes, part time speech therapist

Barry Blake, Chris Cooper and Bernadette Church. In 1995 Mr. Blake's second and third graders made a videotape of songs about California that they sent to their penpals in Chicago.[80]

Ms. Mullan's math and science class went on a field trip to study the ocean. Mr. Dana Johnston drove the bus with a stop in Mckinleyville at a carpenters shop where the new Bridgeville School library's bookshelves were being made. "It was awesome," stated Shree Morris. The fourth through eighth class voted as to which color stain the new library shelves would be. Then Mr. Johnston drove the class to Patrick's Point. A lot of the students took off their shoes to run on the beach. "My favorite part was running away from the waves," said Everson Corrigan a fifth grader. Everson and Sean Marshall found a dead fish with hermit crabs all over it. A bunch of people were saying, "Look what I found!" Dawnette Morris found a walking meat loaf, which is an animal that lives in the tide pools. To get to the bus we walked up a steep hill. That night they told stories around the campfire. "My favorite part was the ghost stories," said Aaron Blendell. They went to Under Sea World in Crescent City the next day. People sang a lot on the bus.

—James "J.R." Dunlap, May 18, 1994

Mr. Carrol created an educational unit organizing his class into designing and building a kinetic sculpture called the "Man Eating Crab." Students participated in the Kinetic Sculpture Race.

—*Times Standard*, June 1994

Construction of the newest classrooms at Bridgeville School in 1993.

Time Capsule

The construction workers building the new school dug up the old flag pole on April 14, 1994. All the students watched in hope of a time capsule being under it, which it wasn't. The workers gave up after they dug a foot down and chiseled at the cement for a while. "I think it is buried a couple feet to the side," said Kenny Lee, a 7th grader. Others agreed with Lee. Many kids believed that the time capsule is still there. "I think it's still there," said Gabe Guerriero who is in 7th grade. "I think the time capsule was a fantastic hoax," said Daniel Hamb, an 8th grader.

—Patrick Hamb, May 18, 1994

It wasn't known at the time when J.R. and Patrick wrote their reports for Ms. Taborski, that the bits and pieces on top of an old cupboard in the office were all that remained of the time capsule. The contents had been unearthed for new construction, and then charred in the 1978 fire. The sycamore tree long forgotton. It wasn't until 1999, when Mary Brandenburg (Jardin) visited the campus and the author asked if she knew about the bits and pieces Janice Crane had saved. It was then we learned the pieces were all that was left of the time capsule. Ms. Jardin took the last vestiges of the time capsule with her, laminated the pieces into some kind of order and mailed them to the author. She also wrote the story on page 30 and sent it to the author in 2005.

The Kinetic Sculpture insides and crew.

1997 Entrance to Bridgeville School.

Teacher appreciation week in the picture above; beginning on the left and going around the table clockwise: Barry Blake, Marilyn Grady, Jean Reid, Betty Voit, Annie Schmidt, Chris Cooper, Joyce Church, Jeanie Card, Lori Sheline, Mary Ann Bywater, Barbara Brightman, Rita Leeseman, Linda Griesbach, Annette Church and Kathy Wood. Between the tables: Dana Johnston, Corinne Fearrian, Mike Grady and Julie Hague-Gray.

1995-1996[81]   Management Team Years   **1996-1997**[82]

Kathy Wood, K-2 and lead-administrator
Corinne Fearrien, K-3
Chris Cooper, 4-5
John Blakely, 6-8
Virginia Howard Mullan, 6-8
Nina Kayes, speech therapist
Rachel Owen, music teacher
Nancy French, reading teacher
Julie Hague Gray, special education teacher
Lori Sheline, yearbook advisor
Jeanie Card, yearbook advisor

1997-1998[83]

John Blakely, lead-Administrator
Julie Hague Gray, special education teacher
Chris Cooper, K-2
Corinne Fearrien, 3-4
John Blakely, 5-6 with 16 5th graders and 12 6th graders
Virginia Howard Mullan, 7-8
First day enrollment: 86.

1997-1998 Mr. Blakey grades 5 & 6. Front row: Janine Carmona, Matt Asbury, Peter Saler, Travis Fuller, Weston Gunderson, Ashley O'Meara. Row 2: Mr. Blakely, Andrea Davis, Sierra Higgins, Jessie King, Mark Gladding, Eddie Brinson, Bryan Smith. Row 3: Amy Adams, Troy Brinson, Autumn Johnston, Matt Van Heldon, Bodhi Tree, Shawn Tillman, Barbie Newberry. Row 4: Joelyn Waters, Nathan Myers, Rebecca Ackley, Becky Newberry, Erin Keyser, Lonnie Smith, Kristine Dunlap. Absent: Kimberly Comarsh, Brendan Byrd and Avela Erickson. Taken in the Gordon Crane Gym.

1997-1998 Mrs. Mullan and Mr. Mullan grades 7 & 8. Front Row: Britney O'Meara,
Eli Harder, Deja Bryant, Rachel Haslam, Adam Saler, Shree Morris, Kady Spalding,
Rindy Samuelson. Second row: Mike Mullan, Cassie Brown, Carrie Davis, Christy
Trammell, Ben French, Regina Adams, Jessica Heald, Jolene Card, Row 3: Katy
Keyser, Bethany Keener, Celeste Guerriero, Louie Meyers, Summer Honeycutt, Shane
Davis, Kathy Loveless. Mrs. Mullan was absent at the hospital having Michaelyn.
Picture taken in the Gordon Crane Gym.

1998-1999[84] Management Team
>   John Blakely, lead-administrator and 4-6
>   Nancy French, co-administrator, Miller-Unruh and independent
>   study
>   Rachel Owen, executive committee, 4-6 and band and chorus
>   Chris Cooper, K-2, basketball coach and guitar teacher
>   Corrine Fearrien, 2-4
>   Virginia Howard Mullan, 6-8
>   Carilyn Goldammer, resource specialist and Miller-Unruh Reading
>   Keely Spalding, speech therapist
>   Loreen Farrell, administrative assistant
>   Denise O'Meara, classified representative of management team
>   Dee Keyser, parent representative of management team
>   Carol Honeycutt, parent representative of management team
>   Pamella Barban, parent representative of management team
>   Dave Vegliano, community center coordinator
>   Dona Blakely, yearbook advisor
>   First day enrollment: 86.
>   Some of the best things about this year were Friday Electives,
>   the dances and the mirror ball.

—Erin Keyser

Walt Mendenhall (pictured left next to Jessie Wheeler) retires after 47 years of service. Walt delivered mail, milk, fresh fruits & vegetables, and even Christmas presents to Bridgeville School for 47 years. Gordy, Pam Walker and Ceci, in the top right picture, attend his small retirement ceremony.

1999-2000[85] Management Team
    John Blakely, lead-administrator and 6-7
    Nancy French, co-administrator and Miller-Unruh Reading
    Rachel Owen, executive committee, 4-6 and music teacher
    Chris Cooper, K-1
    Corinne Fearrien, 2-3
    Virginia Howard Mullan, 7-8
    Carilyn Goldammer, resource specialist and Miller-Unruh Reading
    Keely Spalding, speech therapist
    Loreen Farrell, administrative assistant
    Denise O'Meara, classified representative of management team
    Dee Keyser, parent representative of management team
    Carol Honeycutt, parent representative of management team
    Pamella Barban, parent representative of management team
    David Ackley, custodian and bus driver
    Wanda Ackley, Head Start assistant teacher
    Sarah Bender, custodian
    Diana Bennett, Americorp worker
    Jeanie Card, instructional and speech aide
    Lori Carmona, bus driver and custodian
    Annette D. Church, special education aide
    Joyce Church, Head Start teacher
    Lauri Church, Americorps worker
    Liz Dunlap, school board member
    Mike Gladding, school board member
    Dana Johnston, MOT supervisor and instructional aide
    Amy Kirkman, school board member
    David Marshall, computer tech support
    Tim McCollister, sheriff and classroom volunteer

Barbara Mendonca, classroom aide
Corrine Oliveira, EMHI aide
Denise O'Meara, office and noon duty aide
Lauri Rose, home health nurse
Orinda (Rindy) Samuelson, instructional aide
Lori Sheline, instructional aide
Nan Sickle-Mabry, counselor
Suzanne Smith, substitute teacher
Sherri Snelgrove (Wight), administrative assistant
Rose Valentine, librarian
Dave Vegliano, community center coordinator
Pam Walker, cook
First day enrollment: 94.

Learning in the greenhouse with Ms. Sheline.

Bridgeville School Staff 1999-2000. Front row: Annette Church, Joyce Church, Denise O'Meara, Rose Valentine, Chris Cooper, Lauri Rose. Standing in back: Keely Spalding, Virginia Howard Mullan, Jeanie Card, Corinne Fearrien, Nancy French, Rachel Owen, Wanda Ackley, Dave Ackley and Lori Sheline. Not pictured: John Blakely, lead-administrator and grades 6/7 teacher, Carilyn Goldammer, resource specialist and Miller-Unruh Reading and Sherri Snelgrove (Wight), administrative assistant. Picture in front of "monkey bars."

2001   BRIDGEVILLE ELEMENTARY SCHOOL   2002
MS. MULLAN & MS. CHURCH - GRADES 7 & 8

Front row: Michael Sturgess, Ms. Smith, Ms. Church, India Schill, Sonrize Comarsh, Cassie Carmona, Kelly Fleek, Mr. Johnston, Sean Byrd and Allen Steinwand. Row 2: Dustin Johnston, Adam Churchill, Ms. Mullan, Jamie King, Shannel Tillman and Tracy Ackley. Row 3: Ray Rigby, Danny King, Cameron Houston, Mitchell Asbury, Chris Bender and Tim Glass.

2000-2001 Management Team
John Blakely, lead-administrator
Nancy French, co-administrator and Mill-er-Unruh Reading
Sherri Wight, administrative assistant
Carilyn Goldammer, special education
Chris Cooper, K-2 first trimester
Amber Bartlett, K-2 second and third tri-mesters
Corinne Fearrien, 3-4
Rachel Owen, 5-6, band and chorus
Virginia Howard Mullan, 7-8
Keely Spalding, speech therapist
Pam Walker, cook and student council advisor
Dona Blakely, yearbook advisor
First day enrollment: 71.

Mrs. Mullan, Mr. Blakely and Mr. Tillman.

2001-2002
Suzanne Smith, superintendent/principal
Nancy French, Miller-Unruh Reading teacher* and co-administrator
Corinne Fearrien, K-3

Rachel Owen, 4-6 and music teacher
Virginia Howard Mullan, 7-8
Dana Johnston, science teacher
Carilyn Goldammer, special education teacher
Keely Spalding, speech therapist

Support & Staff

Dave Ackley, custodian and bus driver
Wanda Ackley, Head Start assistant teacher
Sarah Bender, substitute aide
Monica Schill, yearbook advisor
Diana Bennett, coach and substitute aide
Jeanie Card, instructional and speech aide
Lori Carmona, bus driver
Annette D. Church, special education aide
Dan Dula, HSU math tutor
Michelle Dunham, administrative assistant
Liz Dunlap, school board member
Joyce Church, Head Start teacher
Debbie Elam, consultant
Loreen Farrell, consultant
Mike Gladding, school board member
Betty Heaton, school board member
Patty Hess, home health nurse
Dana Johnston, MOT supervisor and instructional aide
David Marshall, computer tech support
Tim McCollister, sheriff
Judith Newberry, community center van driver
Corrine Oliveira, EMHI aide
Denise O'Meara, secretary
Mike Mullan, administrative assistant
Lauri Rose, volunteer
Rose Valentine, librarian
Orinda (Rindy) Samuelson, substitute instructional aide
Monica Schill, school board member
Lori Sheline, instructional aide
Dave Vegliano, community center coordinator
Brandi Vitgenos, substitute aide
Pam Walker, cook and student council advisor
First day enrollment: 55.

Bridgeville School Mission Statement

To teach students the academic, social and thinking skills necessary to become citizens who accept challenges, take responsibility for personal choices and value themselves and others in a diverse world.

2002-2003

Mike Mullan and Suzanne Smith, superintendent/principals
Nancy French, reading specialist*
Corinne Fearrien, K-3
Rachel Owen, 3-5
Virginia Howard Mullan, 6-8
Deborah Sypher, special education teacher
Tomoko Akyiama, Japanese language and culture teacher
Diana Bennett, coach
Laurie Church, coach
Pam Walker, cook
First day enrollment: 66.
The school spends $18,000.00 on utilities.

2003-2004

Mike Mullan, superintendent/principal
Nancy French, reading specialist*
Corinne Fearrien, K-2
Rachel Owen, 3-5
Virginia Howard Mullan, 6-8
Deborah Sypherd, special education teacher
Keely Spalding, fall speech teacher
Chris Doane, speech language pathologist 1/12/2004

Suzanne Smith played many roles at Bridgeville School. As a retired principal/superin-
tendent from down south she started substituting at Bridgeville School. Then she was
hired as a long-term sub, principal/superintendent, GATE teacher (Wordly Wise), special
education teacher and then back to substituting. She helped out wherever and whenever
she could, she even ran the scoreboard for volleyball and basketball games in the gym.

Mr. Mullan and students build a new bell "tower" to house the bell that hung in the old school, pictured on page 17. This is one of the many projects that were funded by School to Career funds. Supervised students also built the deck, playhouse and recycling center. In the picture to the right, Ms. Mullan, Mr. Blakely and Joyce Church all take a turn ringing the bell; which hasn't been rung since 1984.

2003-2004 Support & Staff

David Ackley, custodian and bus Driver
Wanda Ackley, Head Start assistant teacher
Diana Bennett, coach
Jeanie Card, instructional and speech aide
Lori Carmona, bus driver
Annette D. Church, special education aide
Joyce Curch, Head Start teacher
Michelle Dunham, administrative assistant
Patty Ferguson, substitute aide
Brooke Johnston, instructional aide
Dana Johnston, instructional aide
Rafika Ramill from Indonesia
Yagmur Kan from Turkey
Lisa Schmann from Germany
Marta Andreoli from Italy
Ann Matula, meets with KEET TV
Suzanne Smith, substitute teacher
Rose Valentine, librarian
Susan Kohl, librarian
Jessica Springer, staff
Pam Walker, cook
First day enrollment: 55.
There were twelve field trips this year:

1. Beach Day at the South Jetty (Parent volunteers are Shannon Putnam, Paul Jager, Sara Bender, Marla Huston and Patty Ferguson). 2. Pumpkin Patch 3. Grizzly Creek 4. Blue Ox 5. Caroling 6. Gate Academy 7. Honor Band 8. Fort Humboldt 9. Wolf Creek 10. Faulk 11. Medieval Festival 12. Pamplin Grove.

The Student Council was very active in sponsoring Red Ribbon Week, a Back-to-School Dance, a Hawaiian Dance, a Valentine's Day Dance, a Graduation Dance and Jump Rope for Heart. Ms. Owen brings snow to the playground in the back of her pick-up. Guest Speakers included poet Joan B. Graham, Buckle Bear, Dan O'Gara telling Irish Stories, the Chamber Readers, Nova Cramer, the "Button Lady" who taught history through the buttons she collected. Kids earned bonus bucks for being caught doing the right thing. Students participated in Monday Electives, Banking Days on Wednesday, the Scholastic Book Fair, the Halloween Costume Parade, the Halloween Carnival, the Thanksgiving Feast and a big Hunger Awareness lunch learning about food insecurities in other nations. Students attended the Community Center Health Fair in the gym. Students continued to learn through long term projects such as the Science Fair and History Day competitions. Last day of school: Thursday, June 17, 2004.

Student Council's community service project of washing the school buses. From left to right back row: Zach, Patricia, Robert, Maria, Brittany; front row: Matalie, Samantha and Elizabeth.

A jello-sucking contest sponsored by the Student Council. From left to right: Jordan Clark, Calvin Comarsh, unknown student, Ms. French, Mr. Mullan, Cassie Lewis and Brittany Henson.

2004-2005
Mike Mullan, superintendent/principal
Nancy French, reading specialist*
Corinne Fearrien, K-2
Rachel Owen, 3-5 and yearbook advisor
Chris Cooper, advanced music teacher
Virginia Howard Mullan, 6-8
Deborah Sypherd, resource specialist
Tomoko Nagae, Japanese language and culture teacher
Chris Doane, speech language pathologist

2004-2005 Support & Staff
David Ackley, custodian and bus Driver
Wanda Ackley, Head Start assistant teacher
Sarah Bender, substitute aide and substitute cook
Diana Bennett, coach
Jeanie Card, instructional and speech aide
Lynda Cesaretti, community center coordinator
Annette D. Church, special education aide
Joyce Church, Head Start teacher and school board president
Lauri Church, coach
Michelle Dunham, CBO/administrative assistant
Patty Ferguson, utility worker
Dan Fuller, spelling volunteer
Lena Fuller, spelling volunteer
Mike Gladding, school board member
Shelly Gleason, substitute bus driver

Mike Guerriero, school board president
Attila Gyenis, community center van driver
Betty Heaton, School Board Member
Patty Hess, home health nurse
Dana Johnston, classroom assistant and water monitor
Rita Leeseman, HCOE nurse
Ted Lichti, community center administrative assistant
Christine Marney, substitute bus driver
Ann Matula, family outreach coordinator
Mike Mullan, bus driver
Rosie Slentz, board member
Suzanne Smith, substitute teacher
Rose Valentine, librarian
Pam Walker, cook, booster club enthusiast and student council advisor
First day enrollment: 56.

This is the year the school had solar panels installed. The whole school boarded the Lady Washington, a tall ship visiting Humboldt Bay. It snowed during recess! The upper grades went to Wolf Creek, Weaverville and the Joss House. Students participated in Honor Band, the Science Fair, History Day and the All County Music Festival. Students competed in both Math Counts and State History Day. This could be referred to as "the year of square dancing," since Ms. Mullan's class taught younger students how

Michael Guerriero, a renowned local artist shown above, volunteered an extraordinary amount of time at Bridgeville School. He taught various art classes, including tie-dyeing, drawing, sculpture, and silk screening. He is pictured with Keisha Ferguson, Michaelyn Howard Mullan and Danny Proud.

to square dance, a live caller, Lawrence Johnstone, came to Bridgeville School. Students traveled to Eureka in the evening to attend
"a real square dance," with enthusiastic adults. Students trekked to
Arcata to teach square dancing to Jacoby Creek School students.

2005-2006
Mike Mullan, superintendent/principal
Nancy French, reading specialist*
Corinne Fearrien, K-3
Rachel Owen, 4-6
Chris Cooper, advanced music teacher
Virginia Howard Mullan, 7-8
Deborah Sypherd, resource teacher
Chris Doane, speech language pathologist

2005-2006 Support & Staff
Wanda Ackley, Head Start assistant teacher
Debera Autrus, administrative assistant (beginning in December)
Sarah Bender, custodian, substitute aide and substitute cook
Jeanie Card, classroom assistant and speech aide
Lynda Cesaretti, community center coordinator
Annette D. Church, classroom assistant and special education aide
Joyce Church, Head Start teacher and school board president
Lauri Church, coach
Michelle Dunham, CBO/administrative assistant (until December
6th)
Patty Ferguson, utility worker
Dan Fuller, spelling volunteer
Lena Fuller, spelling volunteer
Mike Gladding, school board member
Shelly Gleason, substitute bus driver
Mike Guerriero, community center board president
Attila Gyenis, community center van driver
Betty Heaton, school board member
Carol Honeycutt, school board member
Dana Johnston, classroom assistant
Rita Leeseman, HCOE nurse
Christine Marney, substitute bus driver
Elsie Seviour, bus driver
Rose Valentine, librarian
Kru Ting, foreign exchange teacher
Pam Walker, cook, booster club and student council adviser
First day enrollment: 46.

The First Day of School is Tuesday, September 6, 2005. New
Basketball backstops were installed on the playground. We enjoyed a Snow Day on March 15th.

Varsity Volleyball Team vs Bridgeville Alumni: John Hoff, Josh, Savanah and Rowen Silva. Bridgeville players are Michaelyn, Amelia, Courtney, Tonya and Sabastion.

Weekly activities included Learn to Earn banking each Wednesday, swishing fluoride each Friday to keep our teeth healthy and Monday Afternoon electives. The Student Council sponsored a Halloween Dance, a Valentine's Dance, a Karaoke Dance and a talent show. Special events at Bridgeville School included the annual Halloween Costume Parade, the Thanksgiving Feast, award assemblies, STAR testing and the Community Center arranged for dentists to visit on site. Field Trips were taken to the South Jetty in the fall for Beach Day, after school students went to play chess at Jacoby Creek School several times. Ms. Owen and Mr. Cooper arranged a caroling field trip, classes went to see the *Chronicles of Narnia* after reading the book and the eighth-grade trip was to Washington D.C. and New York.

Guest speakers included Robert San Souci, author of Mulan, Chamber Readers, Arts and Crafts with Patty Kendrick, story tellers Dan O'Gara, Don Keding and Diane Ferlatte. Students enjoyed a Christmas show by Dell' Arte. Our foreign exchange teacher, Kru Ting, was from Thailand.

Students competed in the Bus Poster Contest, the National Geographic Bee, Math Counts, History Day, the Science Fair and the Spelling Bee. Students participated in both a fall and a spring Field Day, Jump Rope for Heart, a Read-a-thon and square dancing.

Last day of school: Friday, June 23, 2006.

2006-2007
   Mike Mullan, superintendent/principal
   Nancy French, reading specialist*
   Corinne Fearrien, K-2
   Rachel Owen, 3-4-5
   Virginia Howard Mullan, 6-8
   Suzanne Smith, resource specialist
   Chris Doane, speech language pathologist
2007-2008
   Mike Mullan, superintendent/principal
   Nancy French, reading specialist
   Corinne Fearrien, K-3
   Rachel Owen, 4-6
   Virginia Howard Mullan, 7-8
   Suzanne Smith, resource specialist
   Chris Doane, speech language pathologist
2008-2009
   Mike Mullan, superintendent/principal
   Nancy French, reading specialist
   Corinne Fearrien, K-2
   Rachel Owen, 3-5
   Virginia Howard Mullan, 6-8
   Suzanne Smith, special education
   Chris Doane, speech language pathologist

Ms. Owen in her classroom.

Ms. Owen teaching a lesson with the solar oven.

2009-2010
> Mike Mullan, superintendent/principal
> Nancy French, reading specialist
> Corinne Fearrien, K-2
> Rachel Owen, 3-5
> Virginia Howard Mullan, 6-8
> Suzanne Smith, resource specialist
> Chris Doane, speech language pathologist

2010-2011
> Mike Mullan, superintendent/principal
> Corinne Fearrien, K-2
> Rachel Owen, 3-5
> Virginia Howard Mullan, 6-8
> Suzanne Smith, resource specialist
> Chris Doane, speech language pathologist
> Tidbits of interest were Zumba, Health Fair, Tour of the Unknown Coast, Volleyball, pumpkin patch, story teller Charlie Chin and Dell' Arte.

2011-2012
> Mike Mullan, superintendent/principal
> Corinne Fearrien, K-2
> Rachel Owen, 2-5
> Virginia Howard Mullan, 6-8
> Suzanne Smith, resource specialist
> Chris Doane, speech language pathologist

Pam Walker (school cook for many years) Jessie Wheeler (retired school board member) and Lola Cathey (retired teacher, principal, and superintendent) in 2012. Photo by Virginia Howard Mullan.

Support & Staff
> Max Anderson, custodian
> Wanda Ackley, Head Start assistant teacher
> Jennifer Bishop
> Robert Bruce
> Jeanie Card, classroom assistant
> Sarah Carey
> Annette D. Church, classroom assistant and special education aide
> Joyce Church, Head Start teacher
> Clara Cross, school site council
> Curtis Cross, school board member
> Isaac Mikus, school board member
> Traci O'Brien, school board member
> Lynne Reardon, after school harp
> Frieda Smith
> Suzanne Smith, substitute teacher and resource specialist
> Jessica Springer, secretary
> Cathy Stanley
> Rose Valentine, librarian
> Pam Walker, cook

2012-2013

    Mike Mullan, superintendent/principal
    Corinne Fearrien, K-2
    Rachel Owen, 3-5
    Virginia Howard Mullan, 6-8
    Suzanne Smith, special education teacher
    Chris Doane, speech language pathologist

2013-2014

    Mike Mullan and Beth Anderson, principals
    Corrine Fearrien, K-2
    Rachel Owen, 3-5
    Virginia Howard Mullan and Beth Anderson, 6-8
    Suzanne Smith, special education teacher
    Chris Doane, speech language pathologist

    After 30 years of service, Ms. Mullan retired from Bridgeville School. Only the second teacher to retire from Bridgeville. Superintendent/principal, bus driver and water plant manager, Mr. Mullan also retired. After 20 years of service, Ms. Owen got married and moved to teach in Crescent City. Annette Church, long time special education and regular education teaching assistant, retired and moved to Wyoming. Big changes for our small school.

2014-2015

    Beth Anderson, principal
    Corrine Fearrien, K-3
    Joyce Church, 4-6
    Heidi Taylor, 7-8

2015-2016

    Beth Anderson, principal
    Corrine Fearrien, K-3
    Joyce Church, 4-6
    Heidi Taylor, 7-8

Bridgeville campus circa 2016.

Bridgeville school in 2016.

Mr. Blakely

2016-2017
  Beth Anderson, principal
  Corrine Fearrien
  Joyce Church
  Heidi Taylor, 6-8
2017-2018
  John Blakely, superintendent
  Corrine Fearrien
  Joyce Church
  Heidi Taylor, left mid-year
  Enrollment: 14
    After many years of service, Ms. Fearrien becomes the third
  teacher to retire from Bridgeville School.
2018-2019
  John Blakely, superintendent
  Saundi Phillips, K-3
  Joyce Church, 4-6
  Virginia Howard Mullan, 1st trimester, 7-8
  Paul Mullan, 2nd and 3rd trimesters, 7-8
  Michael Cox, music teacher
  Elizabeth Bell, resource specialist teacher
Support & Staff
  Ashley Byrd, counselor
  Laurie Church, cook
  Frieda Smith, maintenance
  Jessica Springer, administrative assistant
  Marty Tavares, classroom aide
  Kathy Wolff, librarian

Students and staff at Halloween costume parade.

2019-2020
John Blakely, superintendent
Saundi Phillips
Joyce Church
Matthew Torres, 6-8
Michael Cox, music teacher
Elizabeth Bell, resource specialist teacher
Ashley Byrd, counselor
Gabriella Wotherspoon, classroom aide

2020-2021
John Blakely, superintendent
Gabriella Wotherspoon
Joyce Church
Matthew Torres, 6-8
Michael Cox, music teacher
Elizabeth Bell, resource specialist teacher

2021-2022
Don Boyd, superintendent
Gabriella Wotherspoon
Joyce Church
Cathryn Guillette, 6-8
Michael Cox, music teacher
Elizabeth Bell, resource specialist teacher

2022-2023
Don Boyd and John Blakey, superintendents
Gabriella Wotherspoon
Joyce Church
Sarah Carey, 6-8
Michael Cox, music teacher

Students and staff at Halloween costume parade.

2023-2024
John Blakely, superintendent
Gabriella Wotherspoon, K-2
Joyce Church 2-5
Virginia Howard Mullan, substitutes for the month of May, 3-5
Sarah Carey, 7-8
Michael Cox, music teacher
2023-2024 Support & Staff
Sharissa Barnwell, library aide
Angel Church, classroom aide
Laurie Church, cook
John Millsap, maintenance
Frieda Smith, after school program

Adults and Kids through the years have enjoyed a good BBQ whether at Grizzly Creek, Pamplin Grove, the South Jetty or right on campus. Superintendents, teachers, board members, parents and community volunteers have all taken a turn at the barbecue. Frieda Smith takes a turn on the Bridgeville School campus just outside the Gordon Crane Gym.

Jessica Springer, administrative assistant
Marty Tavares, SCIA
Melissa Villalores, SCIA
Diana Bennett, school board member
Brooke Entsminger, school board member
Nick Glass, school board member
Robert Smith, school board member

Danny Proud watches Clark Parvis bob for apples during an October colonial unit in Ms. Mullan's class at Bridgeville School.

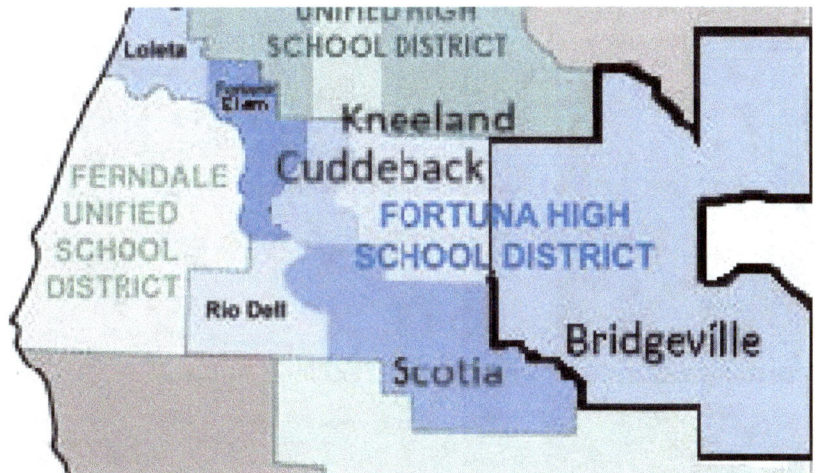

The current Bridgeville School District, on the right is where the district line meets the Humboldt County Line. The white indentation next to the county line illustrates the portion of Bridgeville School District currently being served by the Humboldt Trinity Joint Unified School District. Graphics and information provided by the Humboldt County Office of Education.

The T-Shirts

It started with the Bridgeville basketball uniforms and then in the 1980s t-shirts
became "a thing." Here are a few of the
t-shirts from over the years including some
4-H (after school program) and Community
Center bridges designed by Mike Guerriero.

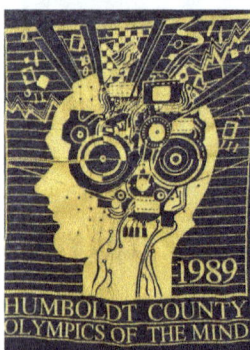

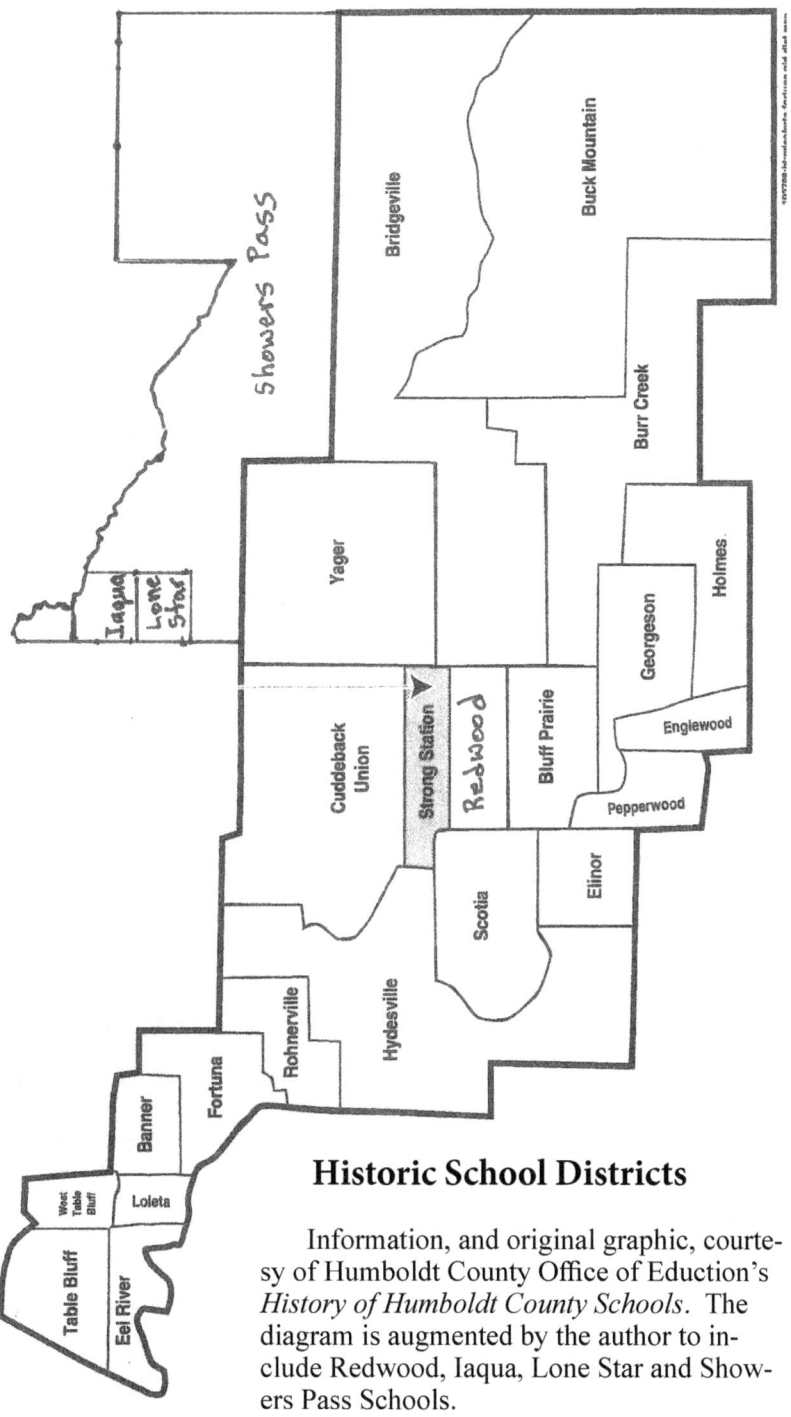

Historic School Districts

Information, and original graphic, courtesy of Humboldt County Office of Eduction's *History of Humboldt County Schools*. The diagram is augmented by the author to include Redwood, Iaqua, Lone Star and Showers Pass Schools.

3

BRIDGEVILLE EMERGENCY SCHOOL

This is all the information we have at this time on the Bridgeville Emergency School.[86] There was another Emergency School east of Bridgeville by Cobb's Store listed under Van Duzen Emergency School, in Humboldt County and part of the Bridgeville School District.

1942

Mrs. Adele Chaffey, teacher

Mrs. Chaffey worked at Bridgeville School's main campus in 1943. There is one eighth grade graduate: Margaret Lois Sutherland who is 14 years old. Graduation Day was June 5, 1942.

1948

Mrs. Rosella Mowery, teacher

Two eighth graders graduated from Bridgeville Emergency School on June 3, 1948: Leslie Milton Marvel age 14 and 5 months and Marvin Philip McCausland age 15 and 5.5 months.[87] Graduation Day is June 3, 1948.

1949

The Bridgeville Emergency School has been moved to the Burr Creek School Building.

—*Bulletin Board*, February 1949

4

BUCK MOUNTAIN SCHOOL

Buck Mountain Schoolhouse, from *Schoolhouse Odyssey* 2012 by Diana Schoefeld. Buck Mountain School was at the top of McClelland Mountain between Bridgeville and Larabee Mountain. Humboldt County Office of Education employed its teachers from 1913 until 1946 when it was merged with Bridgeville School District and all the attendance and graduation records sent there. But Buck Mountain School functioned separately at least until 1959 because we have pictures of the adults and kids there from that time.

1913
   Kathryn Beasly
1914
   Kathryn Beasly
1915
   Elizabeth (Woodcock) Fielder
   The Buck Mountain one-room school house still exists today, albeit abandoned. It's near Deerfield Ranch on McClellan. No idea why it's called Buck Mountain School and not McClellan...
                                                —Oliver Kloseov

   Dorthy Mae Meade graduated from Buck Mountain School in 1937 with a B+ average from her new teacher Mary Catherine Wilson. She had attended Buck Mountain School with six of her seven brothers and sisters all through the 1930s. Mrs. Meryle Hart taught grades 1-8 in 1933, 1934 and 1935. Dorthy remembers that

Pathway to Buck Mountain School.

when they were studying something all the kids had to learn it at the same time. There were 12 students when she attended. There were chalkboards on the walls. Up near the road there were outhouses for toilets, one for boys and one for girls, which Dorothy and her siblings had to walk by everyday on their way to school. Ms. Hart lived in a little house above the school in the teacher's living quarters. Ms. Hart was very nice and especially kind to Dorothy's little sister who was only six. Ms. Hart babied her, brought her special food and made her take a nap.

Dorothy used to walk up one mountain and down the next, about five miles to get to school, but not in the winter because, "the crick got too high." There wasn't any school in the winter and there wasn't ever any homework. It seems like the children didn't give Ms. Hart much trouble. Once; Dorothy's brother, Ralph Douglas Meade, made Raymond Leon Schelling cry, but nothing much came of it.

The students who attended school in 1915: Roland Stockhoff, Allen Cooper, Madaline Williams, Gerene Taylor, Lola Cooper, Dorothy Stockhoff and Kenneth Stockhoff. Information and photo courtesy of Polly Kinsinger.

Dorothy remembers wearing jeans or "any old thing" to school. Ms. Hart wore a dress and so did the Mc-Clellan girls (Martha, Harriet and Ruth), who were daughters of "the wealthy rancher." There were three of them and it seemed like they always had something good in their lunches, like oranges. Dorothy's

Buck Mountain School neglected from years of disuse.

family was poorer and she had apples and dried bread in her lunches. Dorothy remembers a big bin in her home, at least four feet long, full of apples her dad bought in Ferndale and huge 100-pound bags of potatoes and a bin of carrots that her dad bought in Loleta. Once the snow and rain of winter started, there wasn't any traveling to town to get supplies. Those apples kept all winter.

The school didn't have electricity. Neither did Dorothy's home. Her Mom and Dad began homesteading two parcels, 40 acres each. All they had to do was make improvements on the land to keep the parcels, which amounted to cutting down the trees. It was a lot of work and eventually her family gave up one of the parcels. Later on, after Dorothy moved away from home at the age of 14, her dad traded his parcel on Buck Mountain for some land at Fox Creek.[88]

Photo of Buck Mountain School in 1916. Courtesy of Jessie Wheeler.

1916
Elizabeth (Woodcock) Fielder
1917
Ethel Smith
1918
Ethel Smtih
1919
Caltha Robinson
1920
Caltha Robinson
1921
Ethel Jameson
1922
Lucille Miller
1923
Lucille Miller
1924
Marguerite Hurlbutt
1925
Clara Tyree
1926
Clara Tyree
1927
Clara Tyree
1928
Clara Tyree
1929
Martha Wright
1930
Martha Wright
1931
Martha Wright
W. E. Freenaty, Rural Supervisor
1932
Carl Anderson
1933
Mrs. Meryle Hart
1934
Mrs. Meryle Hart
1935
Mrs. Meryle Hart
1936
Mary Catherine Wilson

1937

Mary Catherine Wilson

1938

Mary Catherine Wilson

1939

Anne Ritchie

1940

Mary Catherine Wilson

1941

Humboldt County School's *Bulletin Board* publication lists Buck Mountain as a school still in service.[89] But no teacher is listed for 1941 or 1942. Possibly Mrs. Wright and Mrs. Steele taught those two years from an account by Shirley Schelling Tommila.

1942

1943

Mary Catherine Wilson

1944

Mary Catherine Wilson

1945

Mary Catherine Wilson

1946

Mary Catherine Wilson

A recent picture taken in the early 2000s of Buck Mountain School. As with all the one room school houses they have fallen into disrepair. Les Barnwell said it wasn't worth walking to the Burr Creek School because it was so dilapidated and the roof fell in. Courtesy of Oliver Kloseov.

1947
  Rita Hopper
1948
  Sadie Blake
1949
  Don Williams
1950
  Don Williams
1951
  James Hunt
1952
  Anita Mitchell
1953
  Tom Viracola
1954
  Tom Viracola
1955
  Elsa Lipscomb
1956
  Charles Coon
1957
  Emma Galloway
1958
  Ruth Bowermaster
1959
  Ruth Bowermaster
1960
1961

Anita Mitchell, taught at Buck Mountain in 1952. Then she transfered to Bridgeville School's main campus teaching grades 5/6 and becoming the principal.

Buck Mountain Schoolhouse from *Schoolhouse Odyssey* 2012 by Diana Schoefeld.

I attended Buck Mountain School from 1941-1949. Usually there were a dozen or so students in school but during the winter months due to so many sawmills in the area, we had 25 or more students, making it very crowded. The year I graduated there were only four of us: Graham and Cynthia Cottrell, Larry Davenport and myself.

—Shirley Schelling Tommila

The pupils of the Buck Mountain School had an Easter egg hunt under the direction of their teacher, Don Williams, on Thursday, March 15, 1951. Parents assisting were Mrs. Voight and Mrs. Crabb.

Prizes were awarded to those collecting the largest and the least number of eggs, as well as to those finding certain numbered eggs.

Those receiving prizes were Beverly Coffer, Cynthia Cottrell, Darlene McCombs, Harold Coffer, David Voight, Rick Voight, Gene Voight and Dick Crabb.

In conjunction with the Easter party, Gene Voight celebrated his 12th birthday. A beautifully decorated cake was provided by Mrs. Voight for the entire school, decorations following the Easter theme.

—*Bulletin Board*, April 1951

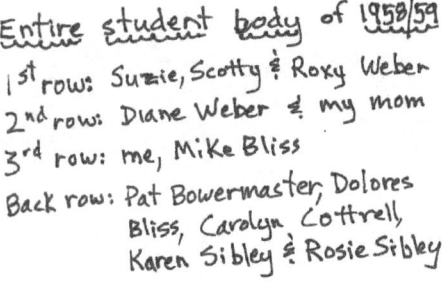

Entire student body of 1958/59
1st row: Suzie, Scotty & Roxy Weber
2nd row: Diane Weber & my mom
3rd row: me, Mike Bliss
Back row: Pat Bowermaster, Dolores Bliss, Carolyn Cottrell, Karen Sibley & Rosie Sibley

Photos on this page courtesy of Oliver Kloseov. Above is the student body from 1958-59 school year. To the right is the 1959 Buck Mountain School graduation ceremony of Carolyn Cottrell and Dolores Bliss with school board member Ted Bowermaster.

According to the *History of Humboldt County Schools*, Buck Mountain didn't close until 1961, but no teachers are listed for 1960 or 1961. Possibly Ginny Metcalf Bowermaster was the teacher for those two years.My dad (Larry Bowermaster) and our aunt Pat Bowermaster Puccetti attended Buck Mountain School in the late 1950s/early 1960s. Grandma Ginny Bowermaster (nee Metcalf) was the teacher, about a dozen kids K-8.

—Oliver Kloseov

Buck Mountain School in 1959.

5

BUG CREEK SCHOOL

A group of students at Bug Creek School with Rowetta Miller's mom: Isabel "Bella" Peterson in the right foreground. It appears her sister Darlene Peterson is directly behind her. Another sister Arvis Peterson is no doubt the one in the front with the white hat and looking down. Photo courtesy of Rowetta Miller.

To get to Bug Creek from Bridgeville, go up Kneeland Road and over the mountain to Butler Valley and across the Mad River. But it is really easier to go through Kneeland a different way.
—Pansy Burke

My Great Uncle Dee Harmon's homestead cabin is where the Bug Creek School was held.
—Rowetta Miller

My mom homeschooled me for first and second grades. For third grade (and until my family moved to Eureka when I was 10) my dad and I rode horses down the mountain to Bug Creek School each morning. Each afternoon he would come and "pick me up" and we'd ride horses back up the mountain to our homestead.

There was an outhouse at Bug Creek School. They had "desks," but they were just tables.
—Pansy Burke

Bug Creek School kids courtesy of Pansy Burke.

Bug Creek School courtesy of Pansy Burke.

6

BURR CREEK SCHOOL

Burr Creek School.

The Burr Creek School District was established on April 13, 1887 (from Inland and Bridgeport Districts). It lapsed as a district on July 7, 1942 into the Bridgeville School District. This school was created for the farmers south of the Bridgeport District, and north of the Larabee District. It was a one-story structure built on the side of a slight incline at the top of a long incline into the valley of Larabee Creek. The desks were small and homemade. The larger children had trouble fitting into them.[90]

1887

Frank Cuddeback

Frank Cuddeback was paid $65.00 per month. There were six boys and six girls in his class. The furniture was satisfactory. The school grounds were unsatisfactory, with too much slope and no improvement. There was one book in the library. The building was 16' by 20' wide with a 9' ceiling. There was no outhouse.[91]

1888

Frank Cuddeback

There are now seven books in the library.

1889

Wallace Feenary

1900

Anna Friedenbach

1902

Anna Friedenbach

1903

Nettie Scribner

1904

Bertha Hull (Bertha also taught at Strong Station School in 1906)

1905

Henry Marvel

1906

Alice Ross

1907

Emma McCrum

1908

Emma McCrum

1909

Sada Carter Wright

1910

Henry Marvel (Harvy Marvel also ran the Bridgeville Hotel for Barnum for a number of years.) [92]

1911

Henry Marvel

1912

Henry Marvel

1913

Mrs. S. M. Ray

1914

Winnefred Menzies

1915

Winnefred Menzies

1916

Ruth Moorehead, soon to be Ruth French

I started teaching at Burr Creek School in 1916. I taught for 16 years, on and off, until the school closed. Once I had three eighth grade students at the same time. I had fun teaching and if I were young again I would teach again." I taught arithmetic, reading and history.

On hot summer days the children always got to go down to the creek and swim or put their feet in the water. They played with spiders and frogs on the banks of the creek.[93]

Sometimes the students would make a sled and slid down the wet grassy hills.

—Ruth Moorehead French [94]

At Burr Creek School the punishment was strict. A child would get slapped across the knuckles with a ruler and they had to sit in a corner in the schoolhouse with their back facing the students if they were caught misbehaving. There was no running water. Children had to walk to the nearby creek with a bucket and bring back water.[95]

—Ruth Moorehead French

My Dad, Philo Barnwell, was the last eighth grade student at Burr Creek.

—Les Barnwell [96]

Ruth Moorehead married one of Orinda and Greenleaf C. French's four children: Alden French. She moved to his homestead which is now part of Chalk Mountain Ranch.

1917
Mary Lanini
1918
Mary Lanini
1919
Effie Rowley
1920
Effie Rowley
1921
Ruth French
1922
1923
Ruth French
1924
Ruth French
1925
Ruth French
1926
Ruth French
1927
Ruth French

1928
   Ruth French
1929
   Louise Lima
1930
   Pearl C. Haun
1931
   Ruth French
1932
   Ruth French
1933
   Ruth French
1934
   Ruth French
1935
   Ruth French
1936
   Ruth French
1937
   Ruth French
1938
   Ruth French

Closing Day Picnic at the Big Rock, Bridgevile School 1937. Top Row: Rollan Smith, James Murray, Clara Murray, Mary Davis, Gene Smith, Herbert Mead, Lucile Leonard. Bottom Row: Miss Evelyn Shuster, Louise Davis, Laura Burns, Glen Davis and Elaine Gleason. Photo courtesy of Evelyn Shuster Worthen.

1939
    Ruth French
1941
    Humboldt County Schools *Bulletin Board* publication lists Burr
    Creek as a school still in service.[97]
1949
    The Bridgeville Emergency School has been moved to the
    Burr Creek School Building.
                                    —*Bulletin Board*, February 1949

    My Dad, M.P. Richardson, attended Burr Creek School. He
moved to Humboldt County from Arkansas. For the first day at his
new school he wore bib-overalls and combat boots. The local kids
all made fun of him and a physical brawl ensued. Dad told me that
he won the fight and all those kids wore combat boots to school the
next day.
                                    —Laura Richardson[98]

7

IAQUA SCHOOL

Photo of Iaqua Schoolhouse, from *Schoolhouse Odyssey* 2012 by Diana Schoefeld. More information can be found about Iaqua School in *History of Humboldt County Schools* Vol. II pages 37-39. Courtesy of Humboldt County Schools.

In the 1860s and early 1870s when the Frame Place was an active center there were 30 students in the unofficial school. Some of the students names from this time are: Ada Frame, Mattie Frame, Dora Frame, Maude Frame, Ora Hunter and Nina Shaw. Some of the teachers who taught at Iaqua during the Frame ranch's busy season were: The Jamiesons (husband and wife) and Denver Sevier.[99]

For a while there was a school in the home of Sam Shaw on his ranch, situated just below the road in front of the Frank Hunter home. Sam Shaw was a trustee and classes were held in his house.

The Iaqua School District was officially established on June 21, 1876 on the road past Fredericksons.

1876

Mr. E. D. Daugherty

His salary was $72.50 per month. There were 17 boys and 12 girls in his class. Mr. Daugherty reported that there was insufficient furniture. There was no water available and, "Some of the desks are splintery!" There was neither a library or an outhouse. Mr. Daugherty also taught at either Bridgeport or Bridgeville School in 1878.

1877

Mr. J.A. Little, first session

Mr. E. D. Daugherty, second session

There were nine boys and seven girls in class. Complaints about the desks and no water continued.

1878

Mr. J. Stringfield, first session

Etta Palmer, second session

Mr. Stringfield earned $70.00 per month and had thirteen boys and seven girls in his class. Etta Palmer's salary was $60.00 per month. She taught twelve boys and twelve girls. A library was started with eleven books. There was a supply of water and an outhouse was built.

1879

Etta Palmer

1887

J. P. Mahan

1888

J. P. Mahan

There was no source of water nearby, but there were 166 books in the library. Thirteen boys and eleven girls are enrolled.

1889

Alfred Downes, first session (earned $65.00 per month)

A. C. Jarvett, second session

There were 173 books in the library. The water source was good. The outhouse was in bad condition in the first session; by the second session it had no roof and the door was broken off!

1900

Anna C. Jewett (Gift)

Anna Gift, formerly a Jewett, tried and succeeded for a time in keeping the Iaqua school (a new one on the road past Fredericksons) in operation. She was faithful and persevering in carrying on her mission.

—Elva A. Shaw

1903

G. C. Rutan

1904
    Sadie Person (taught at Kneeland in 1903)
1905
    Mabel Chase
1906
    Mabel Chase
1907
1908
    Agnes Daugherty
1909
    Agnes Roberts
1910
    Alice Person
1911
    Mary Varley
1912
1913
    Lillie Zimmerman (Drewry)
1914
    Lillie Zimmerman (Drewry)
1915
    Lillie Zimmerman (Drewry)
1916
    Elva Murray

Left to right: Lillie Zimmerman [Mrs. Irwin Drewry], Ellen Bjorkstrand [Sargent], Ray Breeden, Frank Breeden, Harry Gift, George Gift, unknown, Hugh McCord on horseback. Photo circa 1913-1915 courtesy of Humboldt Office of Education.

Some of the children's names who attended Iaqua School during 1916-1918 were: Lois and Ruth Frederickson, Willard Sibley, Harry and Lloyd Gift.[100]

1917

Elva Murray

1918

1919

1920

1921

Lillain Crabtree (taught at Showers Pass before coming to Iaqua)

1922

Lillain Crabtree

There is some talk of the school lapsing at the end of the session, which might be why there isn't a teacher listed for 1923-1938. According to *History of Humboldt County Schools* Vol. II. the school continues until 1938, although no teachers are listed.

1923

1924

1925

1926

1927

1928

The Iaqua School District is 150 square miles. It gets its first phone line in January 1928.[101]

1929

1930

1931

1932

School lapses into Lone Star District, although geographically it became part of the Showers Pass District which lapsed into the Bridgeville School District.[102] Several sources say it eventually lapses into Kneeland District.

Perhaps Iaqua school existing past 1922 is only a typo from the *History of Humboldt County Schools* since no teachers are listed. In one place it says the school was open until 1938 and in another that it lapses October 18, 1932 into Lone Star in the Kneeland District. The latter I am more inclined to believe because of the specific date. It does mention that the school building continued to be used for community activities, such as meetings, dances, parties and similar events. I am looking forward to learning more about this small school.

We used to go dancing at Iaqua School in the 1950s, they had monthly dances.

—Rowetta Miller

8

LARABEE SCHOOL

Larabee School.

The Larabee School started in July. Most schools closed in the winter because of the weather back then. Five pupils attended Larabee School when Miriam Marks taught there.

On hot days Ms. Marks took the students down to play in the creek. Sometimes they played games outside, went on a picnic or other outing. They played tree tag. When strawberries were in season they picked wild strawberries.

—Tiffany Lee

Written in 1985 after interviewing Miriam Marks at Bridgeville School.

Miriam Marks remembers when her pupils at Larabee School collected a jar full of spider eggs. There was a real problem when the eggs hatched and they turned out to be black widow spider eggs! They set the jar in a pan of water so there was a moat the spiders couldn't cross over.

—Stephanie Hernandez and Angie Pitch

Written in 1985 after interviewing Miriam Marks at Bridgeville School.

9

LONE STAR SCHOOL DISTRICT

Lone Star School.

1900
   Jamie Logan
1901
1902
1903
   Mary Mormile
1904
   Maude Smith
1905
   Maude Smith[103]

Lone Star School.

1906
>   Irene Irwin
1907
>   Mable B. Curry[104]
1908
>   Mable B. Curry
1909
>   Mable B. Curry
1910
>   Mable B. Curry
1911
>   Nellie Zimmerman
1912
>   Nellie Zimmerman
1913
>   Nellie Zimmerman
>   Some student's names from 1913 to 1916 were: Ellen and Mabel Johnson, Tommy Dolf, Alice and Bessie Chandler, and a Chandler boy, and a Jones girl.[105]
1914
1915
>   Elva Murray

Elva Murray's salary was $70 per month. There were three boys and four girls in her class. She transfered to Iaqua School to teach in 1916 and 1917.

1916

Inez Cooper

1917

Elva Murray

1918

Emma Newell

1919

Emma Newell

1920

Edith Clendenin

1921

Verna I. Dunn (Pederson)[106]

1922

Grace Ogg

1923

Ellen H. Johnson

1924

Margaret Baker

1925

Mary Lindberg

1926

Ellen H. Johnson

1927

1928

Myrtle F. K. Tabor (Miss Falvar according to Erwin Fredrickson)
Lone Star gets its first phone line in January 1928.[107]

During recess we used to play games like hide and seek and softball. We also went salamander hunting in a pond behind the school and played on rope swings. We cut a three foot diamond shape piece of madrone bark off a tree and used it as a sled to slid down the grass hills by the school.

—Erwin Fredrickson

1929

Geraldine Ford Hansen

1930

Geraldine Ford Hansen

1931

Emily Pond

I had one brother and we rode to school together on the same horse when we were younger, then we each got to ride our own horse when we were older. The school was plain except for the art work or the "good" papers the children did. A stove was on the side of the room by the teacher's desk to heat the room.

—Eleanor Shaw Edsall

1932

Emily Pond

Iaqua School District lapses into Lone Star School District.

1933

Emily Pond

1934

Emily Pond

Erwin Fredrickson, Elinor Shaw [Edsall], and Hi Pond were in my class. Mrs. Pond was a round woman about 5'5" and she stood in front of the room. Her brown hair was tied in a tight knot high on her head. She often wore a flowered dress and brown shoes. She read *Beautiful Joe*, a novel by Margaret Marshall Saunders aloud to us.

—Edra Moore

1936

Emily Pond

1937

1938

Lone Star School District lapses into Kneeland School District, but the land is part of Showers Pass School District.

For several years after the school closed, Mr. Schmalz, a Kneeland teacher, would take his students on a field trip to have them draw the old Lone Star School.

10

MAD RIVER SCHOOL

There were several "Mad River" schools in Humboldt and Trinity Counties. The first school was a log cabin located at school house opening by Anderson Ford, Mad River. Anderson Ford is just over the Humboldt County Line into Trinity County. Some accounts have referred to a Buck Mountain School as a "Mad River" school.[108] Currently, there is a Mad River High School in McKinleyville. The old Mad River Schoolhouse on display at the Humboldt County of Education is one that was closer to Arcata than Bridgeville. The 1941 list of Humboldt County Schools lists a Mad River School. I have included Mad River in this volume because Darlene Whiting mentioned it when she was interviewed at Bridgeville School in 1985 and she remembered Dr. Doris Niles visiting there; which probably helped instill a life-long love of plants for Darlene. Darlene Whiting was a gem who knew about edible, medicinal and Indigenous uses of plants and gave many talks at Bridgeville and other local schools through the Senior Resource Volunteer Program. Her sister, Pansy Burke (quoted in the Bug Creek section), used to help Darlene gather plants for her talks and drove with her to Bridgeville School for a number of her presentations. The author often drove out to Bridgeville School in the 1980s and 1990s and saw these two ladies collecting plants along the roadside on Highway 36.

The Mad River School House was way up past Bug Creek-way up past the Big Bend of the Mad River. There were no roads going to the school whatsoever. You had to either walk to the school, or go horseback. The closest road was two miles away from the school. We lived about three miles away from the school.

Dr. Doris Niles, while in college, came to gather plants and specimens. We would send her plants to be identified, while she was in college.

—Darlene Whiting

11

REDWOOD EMERGENCY SCHOOL[111]

Redwood Schoolhouse, from *Schoolhouse Odyssey* 2012 by Diana Schoefeld.

When I taught at the Redwood House Emergency School, in 1938, I had four students all from the Crabtree family. Our school was one small room with a small anteroom for coats, lunches and storage of spare supplies. There was a sink with a hand pump. The wastewater was piped from the sink underground to a low spot where the pipe extended into a three-foot-wide hole which we called "our little pond."

Out the back door was a lean-to piled high with wood for the wood stove. A fire had to be built every morning and kept stoked if we wanted to keep warm. School lunches were heated on this stove too, mostly good old Campbell's Soup or hot chocolate.

Our school had a battery-powered radio, so we listened to a school music program that came on weekly over station KIEM.

—Virginia Frederickson Miller [109]

Redwood House Emergency School was painted red and the classroom was heated by an old potbellied wood burning stove. There was one swing for the students to play on. They also enjoyed traditional games like work-up baseball.

—Alan Maki[110]

1931-1932
  Gladys Cave
1931-1936
  Margaret Potter Burgess
1936
  Josephine Baldwin
1937-1938
  Eleanore Carrol
1938
  Virginia Frederickson Miller
1939
  Ora Elma Smith Short

12

SHOWERS PASS & HEART'S VALLEY SCHOOLS

SHOWERS PASS

Photo courtesy of *Humboldt County Schools*.

Showers Pass School District was formed February 16, 1898 from a portion of the Bridgeville School District. It opened in 1899.
—*History of Humboldt County Schools*

Showers Pass School was near Coyote Flat not far from Showers Rock. All that is left are rock foundations. My mother and her siblings went to this school in the 1890s. The Showers Pass School was built in the late 1870s by the ranchers in the locality. It was a private school financed by the ranchers and homesteaders.
—Max Rowley[112]

The neighboring families had all worked together to build a schoolhouse under the direction of Gustav Olson (AKA Oleson and later Olsen). A school building was required by the county before they would send out a teacher who boarded one month at a time in different homes on the mountain. Both the Olson and Phillips children attended this school, along with others who rode horseback from nearby ranches and homesteads. The Phillips children walked to school with Carmen Wagner. Later in the year a snowstorm blew over the mountains while they were all in school. The teacher dismissed class early that day so they could get home safely. Carmen Wager and the Phillips children walked in snow so deep they had to follow the tops of the fence posts to find their way home. A few years later when the teacher was ill, Laura, the oldest girl in the school at that time, took over the classroom for the teacher, keeping the schedule running smoothly.

—Naida Olsen Gipson[113]

While we were waiting for the school to be built our classes were held outdoors under a spreading oak tree.

—Carrie Olson[114]

1899

Chas. K. Harper

Harper's salary was $65 per month. There were three boys and two girls in his class. Showers Pass School, as seen on the previous page, was recored to be 13' by 13' with a 10' ceiling. There were no real desks, only benches.

—*History of Humboldt County Schools*

1900

Roberta Fulghum

1901

Roberta Fulghum

1902

Roberta Fulghum

1903

Roberta Fulghum

1904

Florence Knowles

Classes began at 9:00 a.m. and went until 4:00 p.m. (Florence is listed by the *History of Humboldt County* Vol. II page 48 to be teaching at Showers Pass in 1904 and in Vol. IV page 36 to be teaching at Bridgeville School from 1903-1905.)[115]

1905

Marjorie Morris (Woodcock)

I was a first year teacher traveling to my first teaching job at Showers Pass School. I took the stage from Fortuna to Bridgeville and spent a stormy night in the hotel at Bridgeville. The next morning I was met by a young man on horseback who told me to unpack my trunk and pack what I most needed in a pillow case. (My trunk arrived about a month later.) We rode the twenty miles out to Showers Pass. The weather was extremely stormy, and I was glad to get to the Oleson's home where I would be boarding.

Showers Pass had about 15 pupils. The two most prominent families in attendance were the Oleson's (four children) and the Bryant's. A large split log was used for the door step to enter the 15' x 25' school.

The school was made from 10" to 12" logs. There were cracks between the logs, and these were sometimes filled, but the children in idle moments would remove the chinking and leave gaps for the air to circulate through.

The water for the school was brought by bucket from a spring below the schoolhouse. There was no outhouse at all.

—Marjorie Morris (Woodcock)[116]

1906

Maude G. Smith

Frances E. Hood

1907

1908

Robert Craig

1909

Hattie Hull

When my grandmother, Hattie Hull, was single, she taught at Showers Pass. While she was teaching there, she met Frank Bryant. They married and moved to Yager. She taught school at Yager out of her two story house.

—Dona Blakely

First Heart's Valley School left. Second Heart's Valley School right. From *Schoolhouse Odyssey* 2012 by Diana Schoefeld.

Mountain School Teacher Maude Frost, circa 1910, and students of the Showers Pass school, located in Heart's Valley, She is in the doorway. The girl in white and wearing glasses is May Sibley (Salstrom). Next to her is Shirley Ferris (her second cousin). The boy with the white buttons is Ivan Olsen. Next to him, in white, is his sister: Sarah Olsen (Hoteling). On Mike's shoulder is Bryan Saunders. Seated in front from left to right is Ruth Shaw (McBride), Anitia Shaw (Goldschmidt), Clinton Martin, Willy Davis and Vernon Martin. Names courtesy of Humboldt Historical Society. Picture courtesy of Mrs. S. A. Goldschmidt (who is in the picture).

1910
   Maude Frost (Andrews)
1911
   Maude Frost (Andrews)
1912
   Maude Frost (Andrews)[117]
1913
   Dora Brink
1915
   Verna Johnson
1916
   Verna Johnson
1917
   Verna Johnson and Lillian Crabtree
1918
   Lillian Crabtree
1919
   Lillian Crabtree

The second Heart's/Hart's Valley School which was built by Oscar Stapp and A. L. Lamoreaux in 1918. This former school is now used by Hart's Valley Gun Club as a meeting place and a camping stop for hunters in Showers Pass.[124] The new Heart's Valley School was built close to the old school, as seen on page 114.

1920
    Lillian Crabtree (Lillian Crabtree teaches at Iaqua in 1921 and 1922)
1921
    Tura A. Hawk
1922
    Sadie Patenaude
1923
    Sadie Patenaude
1924
    Mary Elizabeth
1925
1926

The original school (Shower's Pass School in Coyote Flat) was basically built for two families – the Olesons and the Bryants. As new families moved into the area, Coyote Flat was much too far for some children to walk. On the first day of school it took the Sibley children all day to walk to school so a more central place was chosen at Heart's Valley in Showers Pass. The new school they started to build in Coyote Flat was taken apart and all the lumber moved. The school was reconstructed in Heart's Valley and given a new name of Heart's Valley School.

Once the new school was built, the old school was used as a home for the teachers. There was a small barn behind the orginial Heart's Valley School that was used as a shed for firewood and storage when Miss Blake lived there. The barn previously had been used for tying up horses and mules during the day when the teacher's house was used as a school.

—Rowetta Miller

The school sat in a valley at the foot of a hill, with mountains and oak trees on the hill that encircled the school in the shape of a heart. I picked the name for the new school. Since it was in the shape of a heart and the 'goofy' newspaper at Bridgeville spelled the name wrong in their paper. It should have been spelled Heart's Valley School not Hart's Valley School.

—Muriel "Sis" Stapp[118]

1927

W. W. Roscoe

1928

Jean Cole Snyder

1929

1930

Winnogene McGowan

Marvin, Muriel "Sis," and Kenneth Stapp; June Zeron and Roy Sibley at Showers Pass Graduation in 1928. Photo courtesy of Rowetta Miller.

Second Heart's Valley School. Photo by Diana Schoefeld.

1931

Winnogene McGowan

Eighth grade graduates in 1931 were: Kenneth Dorsey Stapp age 15, absent 10 days; Marvin Devoe Stapp age 16, absent five days; Ida Muriel Stapp age 14, absent three days; Roy Edward Sibley age 18, absent 42 days; and June Ethel Zeron age 16, absent 50 days. Last day of school: June 26, 1931.

My father Marvin "Marv" Stapp and siblings Muriel "Sis" Stapp, Kenneth "Ken" Stapp, and students June Zeron and Roy Sibley graduated 8th grade from the first Heart's Valley School, on page 110, constructed in the Showers Pass School District. My dad remembered Mr. Roscoe as one of his teachers.

—Rowetta Miller

1932

Alice Jameson (Also taught at Mad River)[119]

1933

Alice Jameson

Oscar Stapp and A. L. Lamoreaux worked together to build the second schoolhouse in Heart's Valley.

1934

Alice Jameson

1935

Josephine M. Baldwin

1936

Josephine M. Baldwin
P.F. Woodcock, Rural Supervisor

There was only one eighth grade graduate in 1936: Beryl Baldwin. School ended June 5, 1936.

Showers Pass School is not to be confused with Heart's Valley School.

—Max Rowley[120]

Although locals referred to the second and third iterations of Showers Pass as the first and second Heart's Valley Schools, the Humboldt County Office of Education didn't promote the name. This is evidenced by the list of Humboldt County Schools published in 1941 which lists Showers Pass as still in existence, but doesn't mention Heart's Valley. In the official Humboldt County Office of Education publication the *Bulletin Board* there are several articles (1947, 1948, 1950 and 1951) about Showers Pass School, but no mention of Heart's Valley School. Graduation Recommendation forms all list Showers Pass as the School. Conversations with Rowetta Miller and Jim McCombs confirm that those schools didn't run concurrently, so my conclusion is that the County Office never officially recognized the name of Heart's Valley School.[121]

1937

Josephine Baldwin and Elizabeth McCombs

1938

Elizabeth McCombs

I used to climb on the rafters in the barn next to our school. When the teacher Bess McCombs, and also my mother, found out she would yell at my friends and I to get down. When it was warm enough we would pick wild flowers and if we were lucky we sometimes saw baby birds hatch.

—Evelyn Deike

From an interview in 1984 by Kyle Ritter and Josh Gatlin

Evelyn wasn't the only student pressing flowers. Hetty Merlynn Stapp had a beautiful collection of pressed flowers. A Humboldt County Supervisor saw her collection and entered it in the California State Fair. Hetty won a grand award, but she never saw her book again.

1939

Elizabeth H. McCombs

Eighth grade graduates in 1939 were: Jane Eveyln McCombs age 13, Carrol K. Stapp age 13, and Marion Eloise Stapp age 14. Graduation was June 26, 1939.

1940

Elizabeth McCombs

1941

Elizabeth McCombs

1941

Humboldt County Schools *Bulletin Board* publication lists Showers Pass as a school still in service.[122]

1942

Elizabeth "Bess" McCombs and Mrs. Sadie S. Blake

When I was in third grade, we made shakes (wood roofing material that is created by splitting thin rectangles from a wooden log) and put them on the roof of the school. There was one outhouse for boys and one outhouse for girls. Each outhouse was a three holer. Two holes were the regular size and one was smaller so the little kids wouldn't fall in.

The biggest challenge for the teachers was that the younger ones were always listening to what the older ones were learning. So, there was a lot of "grade skipping," although the teachers were against it. One little German girl whose last name was Lang skipped two grades and ended up going to college when she was 15 or 16 and that didn't work out so well for her.

—Jim McCombs

1943

Mrs. Sadie S. Blake

There was only one eighth grade graduate in 1943: Beulah Gordon, age 14. School ended June 30, 1943.

1945

Sadie S. Blake

There was only one eighth grade graduate in 1945: Arlie Gordon, age 13. School ended May 25, 1945.

1946

Sadie S. Blake

1947

Alva E. Hopper and Minnie S. Blake (Sadie Blake's daughter)

There was only one eighth grade graduate in 1947: Hetty Merlynn Stapp, age 14. Last day of school: June 6, 1947.

In connection with the study of pioneer life, the children of Showers Pass School, under the direction of Mrs. Alva Hopper, teacher, recently were dipping candles. They had a pan of tallow and by a continuous process of dipping, some candles, similar to those of the pioneers, were made.

—*Bulletin Board*, January 1947

1948

Minnie S. Blake

Showers Pass School has the "New Look" these days. The

entire building has been painted and reconditioned, a new floor
has been laid, a new porch and steps constructed, a new heater and
wood box installed and new cupboards added. Much credit for this
forward move goes to Mr. Oscar Stapp, clerk of the board and the
other trustees of the school who made these improvements possible.

—Bulletin Board, September 1948

1949

Minnie S. Blake

1950

Minnie S. Blake

The Showers Pass School has become a favorite community
center for many people of that mountain area.

The school children assist the teacher and their parents in making favors and decorations for the monthly square-dance and party.

Recently a barbecue supper of venison was prepared as a
surprise and served to 142 guests during the Harvest Dance. Miss
Minnie Blake provides records and assists in the preparation of the
dance program.

—Bulletin Board, November 1950

1951

Minnie S. Blake

Showers Pass School was fortunate in having a newly painted interior this summer. New shades, a sanitary water jug, a cup
dispenser, and linoleum wall covering in the wash area add to the
comfort of the children as well as to the appearance of the room.

—Bulletin Board, November 1951

1952

Minnie S. Blake

1953

Minnie S. Blake

1954

Minnie S. Blake

1955

Minnie S. Blake, principal

Eighth grade graduates in 1955 were: Tamara Ruth Ann Petty,
age 14 and Tanya Iris Stapp, age 14. Graduation was June 3, 1955.
The Average Daily Attendance during 1955 was six students.

One of the highlights of our final school year beginning in
September 1955 was the beginning of our school newsletter, *The
Blabber* whose first issue came out in October. My sister Tanya
was the first editor. Bonnie Gordon, Aron Stapp and I were reporters for the October and November issues.

I had the editor position for the December issue and Tanya

took on a reporter role prior to the school closing. *The Blabber* included a couple of news pages, a society page, notices, poetry, slogans, jokes, riddles, puzzles and a lot of fun pages.

The Shower's Pass School may not have had an outhouse, but the second Heart's Valley had two. The State School Survey Representative in 1955 incorrectly reported there was water under pressure in 1955. The only water under pressure would be if you pressed a button on a 3-5 gallon jug and water came out!

My sister Tanya Stapp and Tamara Petty were the last two students to graduate from 8th grade in 1955 from Heart's Valley School proper in the Shower's Pass District. Perhaps Miss Blake taught from her home after the big storm. We moved after Christmas in December due to the heavy rains.

—Rowetta Miller [123]

1956

Minnie S. Blake

Graduation day was scheduled for June 15, 1956 with Robert Lee Dump, age 14, as a graduate. After 1956 the school lapses into Bridgeville School District.

13

STRONG'S STATION SCHOOLS
Highway 36 mile marker 11.75

The pioneer's log cabin used as a building for Strong's Station School.

At least one of the early buildings at Strong's Station, used as a school, was a pioneer's log cabin built between 1865 and 1870. The cabin was across the Bridgeville Road from a hotel. The hotel was the station that gave the area its name. This was 10 miles south of Carlotta. When first built, the cabin was a blockhouse, and had several square holes near eye level for use as gun ports.
—Evelyn McCormick

School started in July and ran until June. A full list of students and their ages can be found in Paula Gundlach McHenry's book *Carlotta & Yager Valley*. A list of teachers can be found in *History of Humboldt County Schools* IV.

1941
Humboldt County Schools *Bulletin Board* publication lists Strong School as a school still in service.[125]

14

VAN DUZEN EMERGENCY SCHOOL

Highway 36 mile marker approximately 44

Second Location seen above (#1 on map on page 125). Photo courtesy of Peggy Canale. The first school was a log cabin located at school house opening by Anderson Ford, Mad River.

1901
> Maude Beckwith

1902-1903
> no teacher listed
>> Third Location as seen on page 125. (#2 on map on page 125.)
> Photo courtesy of Peggy Canale.

1941
> Humboldt County Schools *Bulletin Board* publication lists Van Duzen as a school still in service.[126]

1949
> Bess Exton

The third Van Duzen School near Cobbs Store. (#2 on map on page 125.)

1950

Parents of the students at the Van Duzen Emergency School held a food sale recently to raise funds to purchase needed equipment for the school. Much cooperation was shown by all the adults in the area who provided food for the sale and purchased items so that a profit of $46.00 was shown in the event.

Boys of the school, with the assistance of their teacher, William J. Achatz, have recently erected a backstop. Also, trees have been planted around the building to improve the appearance of the school site. Future plans call for fencing the school grounds.

Recent field trips have made it possible for the children to collect many rock specimens, trapdoor spider's nests, field-mice nests, snake skins, and the like.

Carl Garner, David Copenhaver, and Marvin East recently caught a young bob cat which was kept at school for a few weeks. Their dog treed the cat, and the boys built a noose, got the cat down and had a cage handy for the animal.

—Bulletin Board, November 1950

1950

William Achatz

1951

Dale Kverno

1952

William Weltch

1953

William J. Weltch, principal

William Nyheim

Kieth Sharpe, Principal, and Mrs. Jean Sharpe of the Van Duzen Emergency School are shown supervising a play period in 1956.

Thomas Edward Blake. age 15, Patricia Jean Townsend, age 13, Hoyt V. Gavin, age 14, and Ben Troyer, age 15 all graduate from eighth grade on June 12, 1953.

1954

William Nyheim, principal

William Fulwider and Frank Hil, teachers

Douglas Stroud age 15, is transferred from Buck Mountain School to Van Duzen in May and graduates from 8th grade here. Graduation exercises are on June 8th. Dale Blake, age 13, and David Copenhaver, age 14, also graduate.

1955

Frank B. Hill, principal

Keith K. Sharp[127]

Jean W. Sharp

Rose Anna Cox, age 14, Thomas Ray Cox, age 15, and Judith Olber age 14 all graduate from eighth grade on June 13, 1955.

1956

Keith K. Sharp

1956

The school was built by the community. They donated free labor and raised money by dances, sales and numerous other fund raising activities. The community, after this tremendous job,

presented the new school to the Bridgeville School District. They
then set about raising money to buy playground equipment for
the school. The community cannot be too highly praised for their
contribution to their school and for their continuing cooperation in
all school matters.

—Keith H. Sharpe, principal

The equipment purchased includes octo-rings, four swings,
slide, traveling bars, jungle Jim, parallel bars, and two tether balls.
The total cost of the equipment amounted to $800.00.

During the warm weather, swimming is taught along with life
saving techniques. Fishing is also a part of the program so that
they may become acquainted with the outdoor sports. Snow games
and sports are taught during the winter to help pupils learn to enjoy
the snow.

Indoor activities are scheduled for cold and wet days. Tum-
bling, rhythms, and dancing are carried on during inclement
weather.

—Keith H. Sharpe, principal[128]

1957

Keith H. Sharpe, principal
Bettie Stephens
Donald Stephens

Robert Allen Danner, age 13, Judith Louise Koteski, age 13,
James Joseph Skriver, age 13, and David Walter Thomas, age 15
all graduate from eighth grade on June 6, 1957.

1957

Keith Sharpe becomes the chairman of a Folk Festival to be held
at Bridgeville School on February 20th. Jean Sharpe also helped
with the planning. The Van Duzen students demonstrated square
dancing to the other schools.

1958

John A. Grisham, principal
John Swierstra, teacher

Gene Ray Burns, age 13, was scheduled to graduate on June 5,
1958.

1959

John and Lucille Solenberger, teachers

1960

John and Lucille Solenberger, teachers

1961

Van Duzen Emergency School lapses into Bridgeville School.

1962

The new Van Duzen School is built in Trinity County.

1963

A flood washes away all the traces of the school building, although much of the playground equipment, pictured on page 123, was saved and moved to the new Van Duzen School in Trinity County.[129]

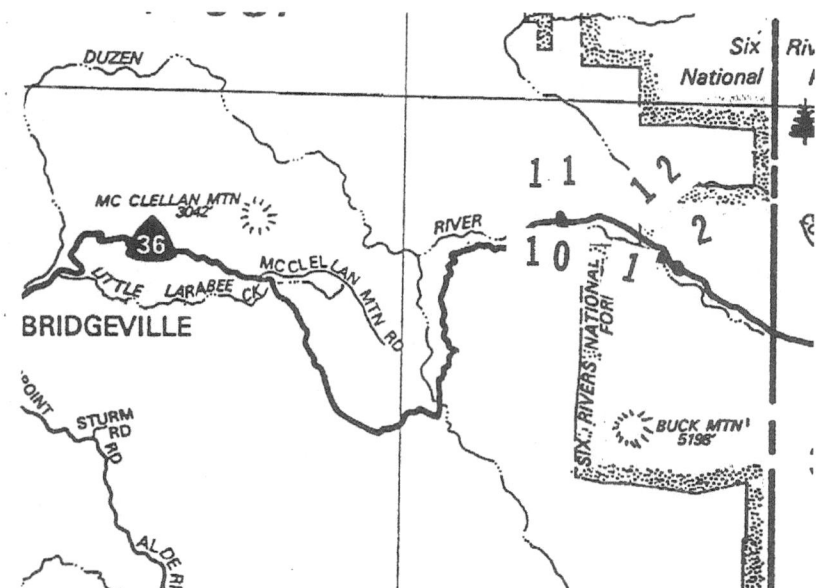

In the map above:
1. Old Van Duzen School (near The Weekender)
2. Third Old Van Duzen School
10. Dinsmore Lodge
11. Dinsmore Store
12. The Weekender
Map and pictures of school #1 and #2 courtesy of Peggy Canale. The "Old" Mad River School and "New" Mad River School referenced on page 106 are both south east of Buck Mountain past Ruth Lake and not visible on this map.

15

YAGER CREEK SCHOOL

Photo of old stage coach stop at Yager courtesy of Sydne Gladding.

1921-1922

Hattie Bryant teacher

The *History of Humboldt County Schools* lists Hattie Bryant as a Bridgeville School Teacher and in parenthesis (taught at Yager). This is the only year that she is listed as teaching at Bridgeville. She went on to teach at Yager School from 1922-1928 with a year off and then 1929-1931.

When my grandmother, Hattie Hull, was single she taught at Showers Pass. While she was teaching there, she met Frank Bryant who she married and they moved to Yager. Hattie Hull Bryant taught school at Yager out of her two story house and then later an actual school house was built and she taught there also.

—Dona Blakely[130]

Yager Creek School was built in 1923 on land donated by Fred Hinckley and Harry McWhorter. It was a one-room school with a small anteroom in one corner near the front door. It was heated by a heater fueled by wood provided by parents in the District. There were two outhouses. The drinking water was supplied by the Bryant Family. Hattie Bryant was the first teacher in the new schoolhouse. Playground equipment consisted of two swings and a teeter-totter.

1923

Hattie Bryant

1924

Hattie Bryant

1925

Hattie Bryant

1926

Hattie Bryant

1927

Hattie Bryant

1928-1929

Hattie Bryant

N. H. Parker, Rural Supervisor

There was one eighth grade graduate: Vilena Bryant, age 14, absent one day. Last day of School: June 14, 1929.

1929-1930

Ethel Loo

N. H. Parker, Rural Supervisor

Photo Courtesy of Oliver Kloseov.

There was one eighth grade graduate: Iness Leona Lewis, age 13, absent four days. Last day of School: June 13, 1930.

1930-1931

Hattie Bryant

Two eighth grade graduates: Genevieve Crabtree, age 15, and Katherine Bryant, age 14. Last day of school: June 12, 1931.

1931-1932

Hattie Bryant

There was one eighth grade graduate: Allen J. Bryant, age 13. Last day of School: June 24, 1932.

1932-1933

1933-1934

Miss Helen McKeehan (boarded with the McWhorters)

1934-1935

Helene[131] Viliardos

P.F. Woodcock, Rural Supervisor

There was one eighth grade graduate: Thomas J. McWhorter, age 13, absent five days. Last day of School: May 31, 1935.

1935-1936

Mary McLellan

1936-1937

Mary McLellan

1937-1938

Mary McLellan

1938-1939

Mary E. McLellan

There was one eighth grade graduate: Benjamin Arthur McWhorter, age 14. Last day of School: June 2, 1939.

1939-1940

Valentina Rocha

1940-1941

Valentina Rocha

1941-1942

Melva Berry

Virginia Endert is the teacher who filled out the Recommendation for Graduation paper.

Two eighth grade graduates: Beverley Beryl Radcliffe, age 15, and Barbara Bradlee Radcliffe, age 16. Last day of school: May 11, 1942.

1942-1943

Lillian Bassford

Two eighth grade graduates: Beverly Yvonne Hansen, age 13, and Richard Harry Sweet, age 13. Last day of School: May 18, 1943.

The Crabtree family who lived about seven miles away down the Redwood House Road (they had 13 children) rode one horse to school at Yager Creek. Sometimes, there were seven or eight children aboard that overburdened horse! Finally, the county built a school at the Redwood House Ranch and the rest of the family attended school there.

—Bette McWhorter Eaton

Appendix 1

THE SCIENCE FAIR

Whether you were a late night, blurry eyed procrastinator or a well organized months ahead type of student, many of us remember putting together long term projects during our years in the public school system. Science Fair projects emerged as icons of long term research, planning and perseverance. Peggy Rice had an exemplary science program for primary students for at least a decade when in 1983-84 school year the Humboldt County Science Fair was still in the fledging stage. There had been a push for a county-wide science exposition in May of 1962. It was short lived and there is no record of Bridgeville School students participating. Some schools, like Jacoby Creek, continued showcasing science projects at their school sites through the years.

Virginia Howard Mullan was involved in the reprise of the Humboldt County Science Fair when she worked at Freshwater School. She was a member for ten years of the county wide collection of teachers and science enthusiasts who met for countless hours to create and refine the science fair as a showcase of Humboldt County's best. As years went by, the Humboldt County Science Fair grew in rigor and size. In 1987 the Humboldt County Science Fair was dedicated to Doris Niles, a local noted naturalist, professor, author of *Wild Flowers of Humboldt County*, and Peggy Rice's mom. By 1997 Dr. Niles' name was incorporated into all flyers and announcements for the event. Every year a student award is given in Dr. Niles' honor at the Humboldt County Science Fair.[132] In the early 2000s Dustin Johnston won this prize for a project about Bridgeville's blue mud. In 2006 Mackenzie Rice won the Doris Niles Award with her project, "How Cineraria Plants Survive Floods."

In 1988, Bridgeville School students "called in" for a Humboldt County Science Fair interview pose with Dr. Niles for a photo. From left to right: Yana Sweeney, Jerry Petersen, Tonde Razooly, Dr. Niles, Samantha Grey, Barry Barnwell, Sonny Simmons and Danny Fidler.

A big thank you to all the judges who judged science fair projects over the years. Mr. & Ms. Mullan, Mr. Johnston, Ms. Cross, Ms. Cathey, Mr. Rizza, Ms. Rice and Mr. Mastaloudis, plus many more too numerous to mention but a few not pictured are Mr. Blakely, Ms. Smith, Ms. Owen, Mr. Grady, Mr. & Mrs. Heaton and Mr. & Ms. Taborski. There have been many more over the years. In 1990, two teachers from Toddy Thomas, Ms. Griffith and Judy Rodrigues, traveled out on Highway 36 to judge Bridgeville School science fair projects as a favor to the author. On their way back home, a rock unexpectedly fell from the bluffs, striking the hood of Ms. Griffith's car and 'totaling' it. They didn't come back the next year. It was often challenging to entice qualified non-school personnel to help judge the Bridgeville School Science Fair.

In 1986, Clint Duey was one of the first Bridgeville School students to win an award at the reimagined Humboldt County Science Fair. Winning second place for his project, "Is There an Efficient Alternative to Gasoline?" Debbie Bowman and Amanda Hunt won fifth place for their project, "Is There Milk in Your Meatloaf?"

Hannah Steinwand conducted experiements about the "Principle of Thermal Equilibrium with Phase Change" with coffee and Coffeemate.

Appendix 2

PEGGY RICE AWARD

Peggy Rice, with her deep appreciation for the natural world, inspired young minds in kindergarten through second grade to delve into the wonders of science. In 1987, Bridgeville School established the Peggy Rice Award to honor her unwavering commitment to science education. This award is presented to projects that not only demonstrate scientific inquiry but also capture the excitement and enthusiasm that both Mrs. Rice and her mother Dr. Doris Niles embodied.

For many years after her retirement, Ms. Rice continued to volunteer as a science fair judge, personally selecting the winner of the award. Projects that conveyed to her "Science is exciting and I'm excited to learn about it!" Upon her final retirement from this role, the responsibility of choosing the recipient was passed on to the panel of judges, who now vote on the project that best represents the spirit of the Peggy Rice Award.

Past Recipients

1987
Rocky Truesdell, kindergarten "Patchwork Tree"
1988
Daniel Bywater, grade 3 "Liquid Buoyancy"
1989
Samantha Gray, grade 6 "Is it Crystal Clear?"
1990
Amber Simmons, grade 7 "Which Filter Works Best?"
1991
Amanda Sheline "Wildflowers"
1992
Jenny Peterson, grade 8 "Horses, Height, & Pacing"
1994
Bobbie Church, grade 6 "Oxygen Build Up"
1996
Bobbie Church, grade 8 "Stress"
1997
Shannel Tillman, grade 2 "Who Has the Largest Feet?"
1998
Katy Keyser, grade 7 "You're Testing What?"

1999
  Autumn Johnston, grade 7 "Bark Making Colors"
2000
  Allen Steinwand and Castleyn Carmona, grade 5 "Dissolving Liquids"
2001
  Tracy Ackley, grade 7 "Did Curiosity Kill the Cat?"
2002
  Chris Bender, grade 7 "Water Filters"
2003
  Beth Bideaux, grade 8 "Plants Need Sun, Soil & Water"
2004
  Paul Mullan, grade 6 "Rock it, How High will they go?"
2005
  Amanda Proud, grade 4 "Burly Burl"
2006
  Matalie Church Nyberg, grade 7 "How do Human Hormones Affect Plant Growth"
2007
  Spirit Tre' Bottom and Cheyenne Moreno "The Deadly Clot"

In 2006 Matalie Church-Nyberg had stiff competition from Brandi and Michaelyn who were "runners up." A lot of "science brings us joy" in 2006!

Left, past winners of the Peggy Rice Award Shannel Tillman and Kayla McKinnon pose with the Peggy Rice Award Plaques. Shannel won the award in 1997 when she was in second grade. Kayla won the award in 2010 when she was in third grade. Bottom right, Samantha Gray earns the award in 1989 seen in this photo op with Ms. Mullan and Mrs. Rice. Bottom left, Paul Howard Mullan, Matalie T. Church-Nyberg and Patricia Bender.

2008
   Jordan Clark, grade 8 "Crumbling Concrete"
2009
   Maria Brightman, grade 7 "Think Twice"
2010
   Kayla McKinnon, grade 3 "Termite Farm"
2011
   Angel Rivera "The Leyden Jar"
2012
   Angel Rivera "Are Ornamentals Invading our School?"
2013
   Sage Roy, grade 6 "An Enlightening Change"
      Bridgeville School has had many winners at the Humboldt County Doris Niles Science Fair over the years. So many that they won't be named here.
California State Science Fair
      The school had three projects qualify for the California State Science Fair.[133] The students traveled to Los Angeles Science Museum to comptete.

2005
Paul W. Howard Mullan, grade 7, Project #J0111, representing Humboldt County in Aerodynamics with "Center of Gravity and Paper Airplanes."

2005
Matalie T. Church-Nyberg, grade 6, Project #J0506, representing Humboldt County in Chemistry with "Electrographic Metal Detection."

2006
Paul W. Howard Mullan, grade 8, and Bender, Patricia Grade 7, Project #J0505, representing Humboldt County in Chemistry with "Acidity in Sodas."

Appendix 3

THE ARTHUR D. NILES AWARD

The Arthur D. Niles Award was established in honor of the father of longtime (24 years) Bridgeville School teacher Peggy Rice. Originally honoring the Girls' Basketball Most Valuable Player it now honors the outstanding female athlete of the graduating class taking into account other after school sports and physical education.

Past Recipients

1985
 Jodie Brightman
1986
 Jodie Brightman
1987
 Jodie Brightman
1996
 Bobbie Church
1997
 Ren Samuelson and Isabel French
2005
 Maria Hernandez
2007
 Matalie Church Nyberg
2008
 Cheyenne Moreno and Hannah Steinwand
2009
 Brandi Church
2010-2011
 Savanah Gardner
2011-2012
 Tonya Jennings

Jodie Brightman with Matt Hunt. Jodie was an exceptional athlete in the 1980s. Photo courtesy of George Brightman.

Appendix 4

THE LAURA PAWLUS AWARD

Left: Laura Pawlus on motorcycle. Right: Laura Pawlus pictured in front of Bridgeville Post Office. Photos courtesy of Jessie Wheeler.

The Laura Pawlus Award was established in honor of Laura Pawlus who lived in Bridgeville from 1917 - 1977. Ms. Pawlus was the Bridgeville Postmaster for many years. She served on the Bridgeville School Board and the P.T.A. She was P.T.A. President in 1948. This award recognizes the overall top academic female eighth graduate each year from Bridgeville Elementary School.

Past Recipients

1976
Jackie Eilers
1978
Jenny Rice
1979
Nicki Friend
1980
Leslie Cottrell
1981
Laurangela Moore
1985
Rosie Slentz
1987
Jodie Brightman
1988

Amanda Hunt
1989
Amber Totten
1990
Tonde Razooly
1991
Amber Simmons
1992
Prairie Johnston
1993
Maria Mann-Gagne
1994
Brooke Johnston
1995
Vanessa Faustine
1996
Bobbie Church
1996
Candy Lapple
1997
Isabel French
1997
Amanda Sheline
1999
Celeste Guerriero
1999
Kady Spalding
2000
Autumn Johnston
2000
Janine Carmona
2001
Erin Keyser
2002
Tracy Ackley
2003
India Schill
2005
Maria Hernandez
2007
Dara Katzdorn
2007-2008
Danielle Bates
2008-2009

Brandi Church
2009-2010
Maria Brightman
2010-2011
Michaelyn Howard Mullan
2011-2012
Tonya Jennings
2012-2013
Cortney Reavis

Appendix 5

THE DWIGHT MAY AWARD

Left: Dwight May at a Coastal Commission meeting in the 1970s. Right: Dwight May and Eleanor May on May Ranch in Bridgeville circa 1941. Photos courtesy of William C. May.

The Dwight May Award was established in honor of Dwight May who lived in Bridgeville for many years. Mr. May was a great supporter of Bridgeville School and served on the Bridgeville School Board. This award recognizes the overall top academic male eighth graduate each year from Bridgeville Elementary School.

Past Recipients

1976
Richie Rice
1977
Don Reed
1977
Walt Eilers
1978
Joe Rice
1983
Eric Johnson
1984
Phillip Grady and David Grady
1985
Ezra Atwill

1986
Ben Johnson
1988
Kenny Johbnston
1990
Ryan Samuelson
1992
Shawn Day
1993
Daniel Bywater
1995
Gabriel Guerriero
1997
Everson Corrigan
1999
Adam Saler
2000
Mark Gladding
2000
Travis Fuller
2001
Brendan Byrd
2002
Dustin Johnston
2003
Sean Byrd
2006
Paul Howard Mullan
2007
Clark Parvis
2010
Tim Smith
2011
Danny Proud
2013
Cedric Silva

Appendix 6

THE W. H. BARNWELL AWARD

Players circa 1984: Robert Houston, Jeremy Boe, Phil Philip Davis, Glen Yarnell, Brian LeRoy, Jessie Hunt, Mike Dotson, Brandon Barnwell, Jerry Peterson and others with coach Mike Grady.

The W. H. Barnwell Award was established in honor of Mr. Barnwell who in January, 1884, located a homestead claim at Chalk Mountain. Mr. Barnwell served on the school board as well as being P.T.A. president. Originally honoring the Boys' Basketball Most Valuable Player; it now honors the outstanding male athlete of the graduating class taking into account other after school sports and physical education. One of the winners took the original plaque home after graduation and it has been missing for years. The award was established in 1967. The newest recipients have their names on a list in the Bridgeville School Office.

Past Recipients

1999
   Adam Saler
2000
   Lonnie Smith

2001
    Brenden Byrd
2003
    Chris Bender
2004
    Zach Rigby
2006
    Michael Tillman
2007
    Shawn Hof and Alex Church
2008
    Cody Iloff
2010
    Josh Iloff
2011
    Alex Springer

Appendix 7

NATIONAL GEOGRAPHIC BEE

The National Geographic GeoBee was an annual geography contest sponsored by the National Geographic Society. The Bee, held annually from 1989 to 2019, was open to students in the fourth through eighth grades. Students stood in a line answering difficult geography questions for four rounds. Only those with the highest score went on to the next round. The winner took a written geography test and sent it off to National Geographic. The only Bridgeville student to compete at the next level was Annie Gordon in 1997 which is why and when the plaque in the library was created. Until 2013, each student who qualified to take the written test (the school winner) had their name added to the plaque.

Past Recipients

1997
Annie Gordon
1998
Adam Saler
2002
Ray Rigby
2003
Sean Byrd
2004
Robert Lewis
2005
Connor Andersen
2006
Patricia Bender
2010
Tim Smith
2011
Tonya Jennings
2012
Angel Rivera

National Geographic Bee logo.

Appendix 8

SCHOOL BUS POSTERS

The California Association of School Transportation Officials (CAS-TO) hosted a bus poster safety contest for many years to promote kids being safe both on the bus and at bus stops. Bridgeville School Students participated and did quite well in the competition. Most students enjoyed the yearly art project (They also improved their ability to draw school buses!). Some winners pictured on the next page are Jessica Wojcik's (grade 5) whose theme was "stay in your seat until the bus driver opens the door," her poster won at both the Humboldt County and California State levels. Paul Mullan (grade 5) and Samantha Glass were both Humboldt County winners. Aaron Sheline (grade 2) was a Humboldt County winner. Other California State winners were Gabe Guerriero, Jamie King and Ren Samuelson. Other Humboldt County winners included: Myla Kirk, Grace Cross, Angel Rivera, Cortney Reavis, Gabrielle Jensen, Devan Morgan, Amber Ward, Tonya Jennings, Amanda Proud and Dara Katzdorn. There is currently a display of school bus poster winners through the years in the Bridgeville School Office. The bus posters printed on the next page are from the 2000-2002 Winter Anthologies and various newspaper clippings.

Cassie Carmona
Seventh Grade

Cassie Carmona's bus poster entry.

Michaelyn Mullan
Grade 2

Melissa Asbury
Grade 7

Sean Byrd
Seventh Grade

Hannah Steinwand
Grade 5

Entries of the bus poster saftey contest hosted by the California Association of School Transportation officials. Aaron Sheline was a Humboldt County winner in 1988 presented his award by CASTO President Doug Snyder. Jessica Wojcik presented her award by Louie Bucher in 1989. Paul Mullan and Samantha Glass were both winners in 2003 with CASTO member Mike Mullan presenting.

Appendix 9

SPIRIT OF BRIDGEVILLE AWARD

In 1994 the teachers felt that there were students who were enthusiastic about learning, always tried their hardest, were good citizens, had good sportsmanship and worked well with other students. When graduation approached in June, they weren't necessarily the best athlete or the student with the highest gpa. The teachers felt that upon occasion this new "Spirit of Bridgeville" Award needed to be presented.

Past Recipients

1994
  Kathryn Dunlap
1996
  Nikki Card
1997
  Linden Wood
1999
  Kady Spaling and Britney O'Meara
2000
  Autumn Johnston
2001
  Peter Saler
2002
  Dustin Johnston
2003
  Shannel Tillman
2007
  Dara Katzdorn, Spirit Bottom, Emily Saler, Shawn, Clark Parvis
  Patricia Bender and Matalie Church Nyberg
2011
  Savannah Gardner
2012
  Freda Hauck and Tonya Jennings

Appendix 10

J.R. DUNLAP MUSIC AWARD

The J.R. Music Award created in honor of and to celebrate J.R. Dunlap's exceptional musical ability. There have been several exceptional musicans who attened Bridgeville whose names you might not see below, such as Alex Kent. Only eighth grade graduating students were eligible to receive the award. The author did not see the plaque on recent visits to Bridgeville School. Perhaps it has gone the way of the W. H. Barnwell plaque.

Past Recipients

1997
    J.R. Dunlap
1998
    Christy Trammell
1999
    Adam Saler
2000
    Autumn Johnston
2000
    Travis Fuller
2001
    Peter Saler
2002
    Tracy Ackley
2002
    Dustin Johnston
2003
    Shannel Tillman
2004
    Robert Lewis
2005
    Cassie Lewis
2006
    Michael Tillman

2007
   Dara Katzdorn
2008
   Jordan Clark
2010
   Rowan Silva
2010-11
   Michaelyn Howard Mullan
2011-12
   Freda Hauck
2012-13
   Devan Morgan
2014-15
   Sage Roy
2015-16
   Angel Church[134]

Appendix 11

HEART OF BRIDGEVILLE AWARD

In 2024 some community members felt that there were employees from Bridgeville School that needed to be recognized publicly for their outstanding service over the years. These employees had been recognized before, but in an unsystematic way. This award aimed to reaffirm the many hours, both paid and volunteered, of superb service that these individuals gave to make Bridgeville School a better school.[135]

Gordon Crane
new gym named after him
maintence
custodian
bus driver

Lola Cathey
Founders Day Award
teacher
principal
superintendent

Peggy Rice
HCOE Excellence in Teaching Award
teacher

2024 Heart of Bridgeville Awards.

Mike Grady
Founders Day Award
teacher
principal
superintendent

Mr. Grady with blackboard and pointer, in what is currently Room 4.

Mr. Grady and I had the pleasure in August of going back to Bridgeville in Humboldt County to visit Mike's first teaching position. It was a reunion for any and all who were associated with Bridgeville School. We saw people who had taught and been taught, been classroom aides, many of Mike's former students and parents. Such a feast of hugs! Mike received a plaque commemorating his years of service. A highlight was a letter from one of Mike's former students writing about "mean Mr. Grady," who stuck with him until he did his work completely, even when it meant he stayed until late at night. John, the student, now a 50 year old man, wrote he learned how to stay with the job until it was done and done properly. What an excellent summary of Mike's teaching career.

—Marylin Grady, December 2024

2024 Heart of Bridgeville Awards with Virginia Howard Mullan presenting. Corrine Fearrien, Pat Sweeney, Brandon Barnwell, Yana Sweeney, Barry Barnwell, Michaelyn Howard Mullan, Joyce Church and Jessica Springer seen in the background.

Appendix 12

SOURCES

Books

Bledsoe, A.J. *Indian Wars of the Northwest*. BIOBOOKS, Oakland 10, California. 1956.

Bucher, Louis. *Ink Wells & School Bells, A collection of stories written by students about Humbolt County Schools*. Humboldt County Office of Education. 1987

California Retired Teachers Association North Coast Section – editor. *History of Humboldt County Schools* Volume II Eureka Area. Humbolt County Office of Education. Spring 1989.

Cullberg, Asta. *The Early History of Humboldt County*. Arcata Elementary School.

DeLong, Harriet. *School Ma'am*. Eureka Printing Co., Inc., Eureka, CA. 1992

Jones, Alice; Richard Krieg, Elizabeth Langworthy, Henry Meckel, Florence Morris, Walter Robb, and Herbert Woods. *Trinity County Historic Sites*. Trinity County Historical Society. 1981.

Humboldt County Schools Curriculum Department. *Early History of Humboldt County*. Humboldt County Schools. 1953.

McCormick, Evelyn. *Points in Time, Humboldt History*. Evelyn McCormick, Rio Dell, CA, 95562. 1992.

McHenry, Paula and Janet Mattson. Carlotta & Yager Valley. *The First Hundred Years*. Gorham Printing, Centralia, Washington. 2021.

Peck, Helen; Oden Hansen, Dorothy Gulliksen, Douglas Nitsch, Velma Titus, and Elma Burns. *History of Humboldt County Schools* Volume IV Fortuna Area. Humbolt County Office of Education. Summer 1999.

Raphael, Ray., House, Freeman. *Two People One Place*. Humboldt County Historical Society. 2007.

Rhode, Jerry. *Southeast Humboldt Hinterlands*. Cal Poly Humboldt Library. 2022.

Rohnerville School District. *Rohnerville, A Glimpse of the Past* Volume 2. Humbolt County Office of Education.

Scott, Lynford. "Looking Back at 90 Years…" Eureka Printing Co. 1999.

Setterlund, Donna J. *Eel River Valley & Its People*. Carriage House Studio Publications. 1991.

Thornbury, D.L. *Humboldt County California's Redwood Wonderland*. Sunset Press San Francisco. 1923.

Tropp, Charlotte., Karshner, Gayle., and Bottino, Helen. *The Way It Was*. Retired Senior Volunteer Program. 1983.

Turner, Dennis W. *Place Names of Humboldt County, California A Compendium 1542 – 1992*. Eureka Printing Company, Inc. 1993.

Turner, Dennis W. and Gloria H. Turner. *Place Names of Humboldt County, California. A Compendium 1542-2009* Second Edition. Dennis W. & Gloria H. Turner. 2010.

Weigel, Lawrence E. *The Nongatl: A Brief Survey of the Van Duzen River Valley from Bridgeville to Dinsmore in Humboldt County, CA*. Area 13. Humboldt State University, 1975.

Worthen, Evelyn. *The Unfolding Drama of Bridgeville, a Former Stagecoach Town*. Eureka Printing Company, Inc. 1996.

Collections

Bridgeville Community Newsletter. September 2001 – April 2024. [Personal Collection can also be found on-line]

Bridgeville Elementary School Site Council Agendas + Minutes. October 30, 1998 - January 24, 2001. [Collection in Binder]

Bridgeville School Classroom Registers. Housed at Bridgeville School. 1950-2019.

Bridgeville School Survey School to Career results. Information for the School to Career program survey. 1999. [Personal Collection stapled together in manila folder]

Bridgeville School yearbooks. 1996 – 2019. [Personal Collection]

Bulletin Board January, 1947 to December, 1953. A publication of Humboldt County Schools, Eureka, California. [Three binders housed in the Humboldt County Superintendent of School's office in Eureka, CA.]

California State School registers for Bridgeville Elementary School. [Housed at Bridgeville Elementary School.]

History of Nongatl. [Personal Collection: folder given to Ms. Mullan by Lola Cathey in 1984 without sources or dates]

Meeting in a Box. September 15, 2003 - May 20 2013 [Personal Collection in Binder]

Recommendation for Graduation completed forms, Bridgeport School.

Recommendation for Graduation completed forms, Bridgeville School. 1927-1958.

Recommendation for Graduation completed forms, Bridgeville Emergency School. 1942 & 1948.

Recommendation for Graduation completed forms, Buck Mountain School. 1933-1958.

Recommendation for Graduation completed forms, Burr Creek School.

Recommendation for Graduation completed forms, Showers Pass School. 1936-1956.

Correspondence

East, Julie. Letter to Virginia Howard Mullan about the flood video.

Jardine, Mary. Letter about the school time capsule and portions that were retrieved from a fire. Given to her by Janice Crane. August 10, 2005.

Jardine, Mary. Letter about A Time Capsule. June 29, 2004.

Jardine, Mary. Email asking for the date of the fire. August 17, 2001.

Jones, Rodney, Personal email to Virginia Howard Mullan December 25, 2003.

Henry Cox & Son. Letter to S.F. Bulletin. July 18, 1916.

May, William C. Series of emails with the author. August 2024.

Miller, Rowetta. Series of emails with the author with phone call clarification. August 17, 18, & 19, 2024

Rainier Brewing Company. Letter to Henry Cox & Son. 17 November, 1921.

McCay, Kate. Information of Larabee Valley Rock and Nongatl Legend. June 5, 2024.

Films/Videos/CDs

Highway Social Fund. The 1964 Flood.

Kahn, Randy. Home movie about the Japanese television show *Bridge to Your Heart* filming in Bridgeville.

Outbreak filming. Filmed in Cheatham Grove. Ms. Mullan's class was on set to watch.

The Bridge to Your Heart. Japanese television show episode about the Bridgeville Bridge.

Interviews

Barnwell, Les. Personal interview by Virginia Howard Mullan conducted at Chalk Mountain Ranch. May 8, 2018.

Burke, Pansy. Sequoia Springs, Fortuna. August 22, 2024.

Campbell, Audrey. A series of interviews conducted by Jessie Wheeler in Audrey's home in Eureka, Ca during 2017.

Campbell, Audrey. An interview conducted in tandem by Jessie Wheeler and Virginia Howard Mullan in Audrey's home in Eureka, CA June 2017.

Campbell, Audrey. A phone follow-up interview conducted by Virginia Howard Mullan. May 1, 2018.

Locke, Anita. Hydesville, California. Personal Interview in his home. 1954.

McCombs, Jim. Series of phone calls with author August 2024.

McKeon, Matt. Bridgeville, California. Emailed questions to answer. 27 Nov. 2007.

Peg. Questions answered about the number and character of the citizens and their losses in cattle. 2020.

Mary Elizabeth. Personal interview by Virginia Howard Mullan conducted at Chalk Mountain Ranch. May 8, 2018.

Richardson, Laura. Fortuna, California. Personal interview by Virginia Howard Mullan conducted at Fortuna EPT about her dad. 8 Dec. 2018.

Stephens, Julie. Personal interview by Virginia Howard Mullan conducted at Julie's home. Carlotta, CA May 2, 2018.

Johnson, Lloyd., and Edna Johnson. Hydesville, California. Personal interview by Virginia Howard Mullan with Lloyd and Edna Johnson at their home. 30 July, 2004. 4/14/2018 and a personal interview conducted by Virginia Howard Mullan at Vanta's home in 2017.

Owen, Rachel. Informal conversation. Crescent City. April 15, 2018.

Schuetzle, Vanta. Informal conversation at Samoa Cookhouse in Eureka. 2018.

Walker, Pam. Personal interview by Virginia Howard Mullan conducted in the home of Julie Stephens. Carlotta, CA May 2, 2018.

Wheeler, Jessie. A formal interview at Jessie's home in Eureka April 27, 2017. Multiple questions and answer sessions/discussions were held both before and after this date.

Wheeler, Peg. Informal conversation. Botanical Gardens, Eureka, CA. June
26, 2024.

Magazines

DeLong, Harriet. "John Brown's Son Once an Important Sheepman." The Humboldt Historian. May-June 1980. p. 6.

Fisher, Rex. "Christmas 1964: The Flood." Humboldt Historian Winter 2014. pages 32-36.

Gipson, Naida Olsen. "Good Neighbors at Showers Pass." Humboldt Historian Winter 2017. Pages 10-15.

Gipson, Naida Olsen, "The Phillips Homestead at Showers Pass." Humboldt Historian Summer 2008 pages 18-23.

Goldschmidt, Mrs. S. A. "Showers Pass School in Hearts Valley 1912-1913." Humboldt Historian September-October 1977. Page 8.

Leonard, John. "Bridge builder Leonard left mark on Humboldt." The
    Humboldt Historian. Mar-Apr 1986. pp. 5-7.

Miller, Rowetta Stapp. "Heart's (Hart's) Valley School at Showers
    Pass, Part I (Closed But Memories Linger.)" Humboldt Historian
    summer 2020. pages 30-35.

Miller, Rowetta Stapp. "Heart's (Hart's) Valley School at Showers
    Pass, Part II (Closed But Memories Linger.)" Humboldt Historian
    winter 2020. pages 30-33.

Nash, Glen. "Blue Slide bridges and their builders." The Humboldt
    Historian. Mar-Apr 1985. pp 21-22.

Snyder, John. "Buildings and Bridges For The 20th Century."
    California History. Fall 1984. pp. 281- 292.

Snyder, John. "The Bridges of John B. Leonard 1905 to 1925."
    Concrete International. June 1984. pp. 59-65.

The Humboldt County Historical Society. "The Humboldt Historian."
    Jan-Feb 1986.

The Humboldt County Historical Society. "The Humboldt Historian."
    Mar-Apr 1991.

Newspapers

Anderson, David. "Bridge repairs under way." *The Times-Standard*. 3
    Jan. 1996.

Genzoli, Andrew. "Bloody Vengeance Marred the New Autumn of
    1863." *The Humboldt Times*. 2 October 1955, p. 7.

Genzoli, Andrew. "Redwoods Country." *The Times-Standard*. 12 May,
    1909. p. 7.

Harden, Grant. "Bridgeville Born Again Believers Build On Faith."
    The Humboldt Beacon. 18 May 1978. p. 3.

Hoover, Kevin. "A Tale of Two Humboldt Bridges." *The Humboldt
    Beacon*. 22 Feb. 1996.

Humboldt Standard. "Outpost of Old West at Iaqua to be 'Hooked
    Up.'" Friday, January 21, 1928.

Knight, Tom. "Artifacts….." *The Humboldt Times*. 13 March, 1955. p.
    7.

O'Neill, Kelly. "New ideas at Hall of Excellence." *The Times-
    Standard*. 12 May 1992.

Nowak, Sue. "Bridgeville man a hero in a fire that killed baby."

Seemann, Danae. *Too many kids, too little space: Bridgeville School
    District seeks exemption from quake code. Times Standard*. No
    date or page number circa late 1980s.

Senior News. "Humboldt School Days." *Senior News*. May 2019. p.
    21.

Senior News. "When Humboldt Goes to the Movies." *Senior News*.
    March 2018. (Do you want a specific article for this one?)

Stack, Peter. "A 'Rescued' Town Has Few Left To Care." *San Francisco Chronicle*. 28 November 1978, p. 13.

The Humboldt Beacon. "Saying Goodbye to The Old Valley Flower Bridge." 3 Nov. 1994. p. 9.

Teal, Janae, and Meredith Williams. "The Elders of Humboldt." *Senior News*. July 2018. p. 14.

The Times-Standard. "A Sin-Free City." p. 1.

The Times-Standard. "Fire destroys Bridgeville classrooms. Makeshift accommodations utilized." April 1978, p. 1.

The Times-Standard. "Water under troubled bridges." 18 Aug. 2007.

Tri-City Weekly. "A new series of historical presentations." *Tri-City Weekly*. 23 July, 2013. p. 7.

Tri-City Weekly. "Heralding an architectural treasure." 23 July 2013. p. 6.

Wheeler, Jessie. "Driving Highway 36." *Senior News*. November 2019. p. 23.

Wheeler, Jessie. "1912 Road Trip: Model T Motoring into Bridgeville." *Senior News*. October 2017. p. 21.

Wheeler, Jessie. "Rural Post Offices, Center of Community Life." *Senior News*. July 2019. p 21.

Wheeler, Jessie. "The Heyday of Bridgeville." *Senior News*. June 2017. p. 1.

Wheeler, Jessie. "The Tin Can Ruckus in Bridgeville." *Senior News*. May 2018. p. 8.

Wood, Susan. "History crosses new bridge." *The Times-Standard*. 24 Aug, 1997.

Occasional Publications

Bridgeville Elementary School Parent Survey. 1998 – 1999

Bridgeville School Ad Hoc Committee. Bridgeville School Change Portfolio. 1995 – 1996.

Bridgeville School. Fieldtrip to Gem and Mineral Show student vignettes. 2001.

Bridgeville School. Graduation Ceremony of the Class of 2009. 17 June 2009.

Bridgeville School. Bridgeville School District Healthy Start Operational Proposal. (date?)

Bridgeville School P.T.A. Bridgeville School P.T.A pamphlet. 1989-19H0.

Bridgeville School. Restructuring Plan. 22 May, 1992.

Bridgeville School. "Student Parent Handbook." 1999-2000

Bridgeville School Winter Anthology. Winter 1999 – 2000

Bridgeville School Winter Anthology. Winter 2001 – 2002

Bridgeville School Winter Anthology. Winter 2004 – 2005

Giessner, Jo. "John Brown's Wives & Children." Red Bluff 2012.

Olsen, J.M. "The Raging Van Duzen."

Phay, Wilbert. "John Brown's Family in Red Bluff." Occasional
    Publication. 1986. pp. i-61.

Smith, Suzanne advisor. The Bridgeville Blazer. Bridgeville School.
    February 1999.

Taborski, Phillis advisor. Blazer News. Bridgeville School. 18 May,
    1994.

Wood, Kathy. Bridgeville Elementary School Background Information.
    1995.

Websites

2009 California Education Code - Section 1920-1924 :: Article 15.
    Emergency Schools. EDUCATION CODE SECTION 1920-1924.
    https://law.justia.com/codes/california/2009/edc/1920-1924.html.
    Accessed July 10, 2024.

Bridgeville Alumni and *Remember in Bridgeville, CA* Facebook Pages.

HUMBOLDT REDWOODS & VICINITY Cheatem Grove.
    maintained by David Baselt. 2008. Last updated 2022. Accessed
    July 7, 2024. https://www.redwoodhikes.com/Grizzly/Cheatham.
    html

Faulkner, Jessie. "Bridgeville goes bidless on eBay." The Times-
    Standard, 5 May 2006. Last updated 30 July 2018. Accessed
    20 Jan. 2024. https://www.times-standard.com/2006/05/05/
    bridgeville-goes-bidless-on-ebay/.

Harmon, Mella. "Virginia Street Bridge." Date of Access 1 Jan. 2005.
    http://www.cr.nps.gov/nr/travel/nevada/vir.htm.

Houston, Will. "Humboldt murder probe: One dead at burned cabin;
    victim unknown, trespass grow found at Bridgeville fire site."
    Willits News. 8 April 2014. Last updated 24 August, 2018.
    Accessed 2 July, 2023. https://www.willitsnews.com/2014/04/08/
    humboldt-murder-probe-one-dead-at-burned-cabin-victim-
    unknown-trespass-grow-found-at-bridgeville-fire-site/.

Lost Coast Outpost Staff. "Bridgeville Woman Arrested for Attempted
    Murder After Reportedly Firing a Gun at Her 84-Year-Old
    Roommate." Lost Coast Outpost. 5 January 2020. Accessed 2
    July, 2023. https://lostcoastoutpost.com/2020/jan/5/bridgeville-
    woman-arrested-attempted-murder-after/.

Humboldt County Genealogy Trails. Iaqua Cemetery Humboldt
    County, California. https://genealogytrails.com/cal/humboldt/
    iaquacemetery.html#Had_Lived_Long_In_Humboldt. Compiled
    by Karen Campbell Hendricks 2010. Accessed August 25, 2024.

Lost Coast Outpost. Naida Olsen Gipson, The Humboldt Historian

/ Saturday, Sept. 2, 2023 @ 7:30 a.m. / History HUMBOLDT HISTORY: The Infamous Showers Pass Murders, and an Innocent Man Framed by Probably the Most Corrupt District Attorney Ever Seen in Humboldt County. https://lostcoastoutpost.com/2023/ sep/2/humboldt-history-infamous-showers-pass-murders-inn/.

The Times-Standard. "Online lecture looks at Bridgeville history." The Times-Standard. 26 Sep. 2021. Accessed 20 Jan. 2024. https:// www.times-standard.com/2021/09/26/online-lecture-looks-at-bridgeville-history/.

The Times-Standard. "Supervisors to consider operating Grizzly Creek park; county to inspect, submit grand jury responses." The Times-Standard. 20 May 2012. Last updated 30 July 2018. Accessed 20 Jan. 2021. https://times-standard.com/2012/05/20/supervisors-to-consider-operating-grizzly-creek-park-county-to-inspect-submit-grand-jury-responses/.

The US Census Bureau. 1860, 1870, and 1880. Humboldt County Population in comparison to Indians. Humboldt County. Accessed June 2017 and multiple times afterwards.

The US Census Bureau. 1850-1880. (I cant read this title but its about productions of agriculture). Powellville/Blocksburg. Accessed June 2017 and multiple times afterwards.

The US Census Bureau. 1880, 1900, 1910, 1920, and 1930. John Burns 7 June 1880 Yager Creek Winfield Lam 3 June 1880. Humboldt County. Accessed June 2017 and multiple times afterwards.

Williams, Trish; et. Al. "Superintendents and Principals: Charting the Paths to School Improvement." Ed Source: Clarifying Complex Education Issues. November 2007. https://edsource.org/wp-content/publications/admin07.pdf. Accessed: July 5, 2024.

The US Census Bureau. 1870. Census in Bald Hills, Humboldt County. "United States Census, 1870," database with images, FamilySearch (https://familysearch.org/ark:/61903/3:1:S3HT-DHRR-FN?cc=1438024&wc=K223-BZ9%3A518653701%2C5 18878201%2C518879601 : 7 June 2019), California > Humboldt > Bald Hills > image 3 of 7; citing NARA microfilm publication M593 (Washington, D.C.: National Archives and Records Administration, n.d.).

Appendix 13

ENDNOTES

[1] Audrey called Jessie Wheeler and asked her to interview her and write up her story for the *Humboldt Historian*. All that happened and I was lucky enough to sit in with Jessie on one of those interviews and some follow-up ones on the phone as well. Spring 2021 issue, page 40.

[2] Not a direct quote, but inspired from the movie *Field of Dreams*.

[3] Naida Olsen Gipson, The Humboldt Historian / Saturday, Sept. 2, 2023 @ 7:30 a.m. / History HUMBOLDT HISTORY: The Infamous Showers Pass Murders, and an Innocent Man Framed by Probably the Most Corrupt District Attorney Ever Seen in Humboldt County. Article can be found online at lostcoastoutpost or at the Humboldt County Historical Society.

[4] In the 1950s a collection of Nongatl artifacts were displayed at Bridgeville School. They were collected from the CDF cite. Allegedly Claude Parrish, a Bridgeville School Teacher in the 1950s, had his students collect Native American artifacts in this area to make displays. Allegedly when Claude Parrish left the school, he took all the artifacts with him. Laura Pawlus was furious. This could just be a rumor, but no one knows where the artifacts ended up if he didn't take them. One source said it was general knowledge that he did.

[5] *Hardships and Dangers of Early Humboldt Life Told by Pioneer.* [George Friend Jr., born July 7, 1856] *The Humboldt Times*, Eureka, California. Sunday, December 17, 1939. George Friend Jr. also attended school by Yager Camp for three years prior to attending in Bridgeville. P.S. Inskip and Mr. Hendee were the teachers there then.

[6] *History of Humboldt County Schools* page 29.

[7] Ibid.

[9] *History of Humboldt County Schools* page 35.

[9] Surveyors often visit the school to line up with the survey marker there under the wooden deck first built by Mr. Mullan and School to Career students.

[10] The Humboldt County Office of Education has conflicting files on E. D. Daugherty. Some say he was at Bridgeport, some say at Bridgeville. The number of students is different for the reports of the two schools, but they both report 11 library books. The County office concludes that the schools might be combined

Mrs. Cathey sharing a Constitution minute and some goodies with Tim Smith, Amber, Michaelyn and Rowen.

at this point, even though they report different teachers and information during 1880-1882. Another answer might be Daugherty taught at both schools at different times of year or that Daugherty was poor at paperwork. The different times of year scenario makes the most sense since according to some old timers when school was held was dependent upon the weather.

[11] From research conducted by Alex Service, Curator of the Fortuna Depot Museum for the 2015 Graves Matter. Alex Service is the person that told Virginia April 27, 2018 that the story of Ellen hitting the Rohnerville man might not be true "in fact" but "in flavor." Ellen was 16 when she moved to Bridgeville. In 1881, Ellen and James Fablinger, their two year old baby, Mary; Bessie, five years old; and another daughter, possibly Margaret, moved to Saratoga.

[12] Van Kirk, Susie. Rohnerville Historic District. Prepared for Winzler & Kelly Consulting Engineers. July 1977.

[13] On January 26, 1881 Mrs. James Fablinger and her family left to settle in Santa Clara near San Jose with Mrs. Mary (John) Brown where her daughter Sarah has already relocated. *Humboldt Times*, January 26, 1881.

[14] In 2007 it was not unusual in California for women to be principals (in 2006 60% of the principals were women) it was less likely in the past for principals or for Superintendent/principals to

be women. Superintendent/principals are often found in small
districts with a few—perhaps just one or two—schools. Scattered
throughout the state, California's 312 superintendent/principals,
based on 2006–07 data: were most likely to be male. Virginia
Howard Mullan checked with Mendie Ballester at the Humboldt
County Office of Education July 5, 2024, and Mendie said the
County Office hasn't ever tracked school superintendents by
gender, as far as she knew, so she couldn't confirm or deny that
Lola was one of the first Superintendent/principals. Virginia
also checked with Colby Smart the Deputy Superintendent on
July 9, 2024 who confirmed this. He also postulated that there
weren't principal/superintendents in Humboldt County before
the consolidation movement in 1946 when smaller schools
were brought together into larger districts. Before 1984 "all"
of the principals at Bridgeville School also had teaching duties.
Virginia Howard Mullan believes Lola Cathey was one of the
first Humboldt County women principal/superintendents because
when Virginia was hired in 1984 it was the first time Lola didn't
have a teaching assignment and was a full time Superintendent/
principal. Lola used to talk about attending administrators'
meetings both Eel River Valley and Humboldt County wide and
talk about being the only women in the room. At Bridgeville
there were three female principals and one female rural supervisor
before Lola Cathey. Laura Evelyn Cuddeback was the rural

Left to right: back row: Leslie McGill, Barrett Richards, Joann Hyrnkiewicz, Amanda
Hunt, Amber Totten, Anthony, Shannon Baker and Shanon Shasta Houston. Middle
Row: Sue Leroy, Tommy Hall, Jon Baty, Clint Duey, Danny Fidler, Josh Sweeney
and Jesse Schmidt. Bottom Row: Julie Morris, Brandon Barnwell, Jesse Hunt, Megan
Bomgardner, Windi Milnikel, Jared Richards, Kenny Johnston and Virginia Howard
Mullan.

supervisor during the 1933-1934 school year. In 1950-1951 Verna C. Fowler Crabtree was principal. 1969-1970 Mrs. Ward was principal. These were all one-year assignments until 1961 -1965 when Mrs. Mary Brandenburg (of time capsule fame) was principal (she taught one more year at Bridgeville under Elbert Burdick as principal after being principal for four years.).

[15] Darlene Whiting in an interview at Maple Creek School talking about her time as a teacher at Mad River School. From Ink Wells and School Bells.

[16] From the *History of Humboldt County Schools,* page 30.

[17] We don't know if they were celebrating the end of the school year but I got a kick out of reading about teachers after hours, "A most enjoyable social party was given at the home of Sherman Lyons (in the Bald Hills) last Saturday night, June 15, 1901. The music was furnished by J.P. Sigsby of Gans, M. Hanrahan of Trinidad, and Miss Josephine Lyons of Elder and was of decided excellence. Misses Callie and Gertrude Robinson of Bridgeville were in attendance." Van Kirk, Susie, "Bald Hills Region and Lyons Family" (2001). Susie Van Kirk Papers. 11. https:// digitalcommons.humboldt.edu/svk/11

[18] The *History of Humboldt County Schools* only has Anita Cox teaching in 1920 but Jessie Wheeler and I believe she taught there from 1919-December of 1921 for two reasons. 1. Humboldt County records don't have anyone teaching in 1919-1920. 2. She was teaching there when Hotel burned in December of 1921. Anita Cox would teach again at Bridgeville School from 1926-1927 & 1953-1956. Anita Cox was Jessie Wheeler's great aunt. Anita was Jessie's grandfather's sister. Ms. Cox Mitchell was one of Laura Pawlus' (Jessie's Mom) teachers.

Mike Mullan teaching science during a Grizzley Creek Field Trip.

Bakesales at Bridgeville School.

[19] Caltha Robinson taught at Buck Mountain School before coming to Bridgeville. She taught at Buck Mountain from 1918 until 1920.

[20] *Records for Graduation.* Bridgeville School. May 27, 1927

[21] *Records for Graduation.* Bridgeville School. May 27, 1929

[22] *Records for Graduation* May 1930.

[23] Campbell, Audrey. A series of interviews conducted by Jessie Wheeler.

[24] *Records for Graduation.* Bridgeville School. May 17, 1932.

[25] From a phone interview with Audrey Campbell conducted by Virginia Howard Mullan May 1, 2018.

[26] From a series of interview conducted by Jessie Wheeler and Virginia Howard Mullan in Audrey Campbell's home in 2017.

[27] L. E. Cuddeback (Laura Evelyn Cuddeback) was Jessie Wheeler's great, great aunt (grandmother's aunt) and is buried in Hydesville Cemetery. In 1906 she lived in the Cuddeback area and said that the earthquake was strongly felt there. Jessie Wheeler interview April 27, 2018.

[28] Worthen, Evelyn Shuster. *The Unfolding Drama of Bridgeville* page 87.

[29] *Records for Graduation.* Bridgeville School. May 19, 1934.

[30] Worthen, Evelyn Shuster. *The Unfolding Drama of Bridgeville* page 14.

[31] Mullan, Mike. Informal conversation in Crescent City. April 15, 2018. Jessie Wheeler in an interview on April 27, 2018 said that she thought both the Richardson family and the Cook family had migrated from Oklahoma.

[32] *Records for Graduation.* Bridgeville School. June 1, 1936.

[33] Worthen, Evelyn Shuster. *The Unfolding Drama of Bridgeville* pages 83-89. The Dust Bowl, was a period of severe dust storms that greatly damaged the ecology and agriculture of the American and Canadian prairies during the 1930s due to severe drought and agricultural practices at that time.

[34] Worthen, Evelyn Shuster. *The Unfolding Drama of Bridgeville* pages 83-89.

[35] *Records for Graduation.* Bridgeville School. May 17, 1937.

[36] In addition to being the rural supervisor for Bridgeville for three years, he also supervised some of the one room schools in this book. P. F. Woodcock was elected superintendent of schools of Humboldt County for the term beginning January 6, 1947, and ending January 8, 1951.

[37] *Records for Graduation.* Bridgeville School. May 9, 1938.

[38] The *History of Humboldt County Schools* lists this teacher as Arlene Delp; but on a mimeographed yellow piece of paper given to Virginia entitled *Former Bridgeville Teachers* by Janice Crane in 1985 her name is listed as Arline Delp. Arline is confirmed on the *Recommendations for Graduation* from dated May 24, 1942 reporting the five eighth grade graduates that year: Lois Louise Davis, Mary Barbara Davis, Albert Russell Hunt, Margorie Anita Shears, and Verna Mae Wilson.

[39] Ms. Fowler Crabtree boarded with the Barkdalls and was a distant relative of theirs.

[40] *Bulletin Board* December 1950. No. 3. Page 1.

[41] *Bulletin Board* December 1949. No. 9. Editorial comment on page 7

Some successful Bridgeville alumni (Michaelyn, Joann, Samantha, Leah, Tonde and Yana) after the All Class Reunion on August 17, 2024.

Some wonderful alumni with Mrs. Rice and Mr. Grady. Photo on left courtesy of Kristin Windbigler.

[42] Crabtree was her married name, after she taught at Bridgeville. Jessie Wheeler was in Ms. Fowler's first grade class in the 1949-1950 school year.

[43] *Bulletin Board* December 1950. No. 3. Page 1.

[44] *Bulletin Board* Vol. IV 3 Humboldt County Schools, Eureka, California. October 1951. No. 1. Page 6.

[45] *History of Humboldt County Schools by high School Districts* lists his name as Ervin.

[46] The *History of Humboldt County Schools* lists her as Eva Stall. But, *Former Bridgeville Teachers* by Janice Crane has her name as Eva Stahl in all instances.

[47] Most schools in the United States are set up on an authority system. Historically it has been hard to come forward with a complaint about a teacher. I believed that changed in the 1990s when inter-district transfers between schools became the norm on Highway 36. So I'd like to protect my source concerning this complaint about Ms. Stahl. Interview May 8, 2018.

[48] Schuetzle, Vanta. Informal conversation Samoa Cookhouse, Eureka. April 14, 2018.

[49] The *History of Humboldt County Schools* Volume IV only lists Don K. Williams as teaching until 1952. The Bridgeville School Change Portfolio has a typo referring to him as Don D. Williams, and also only teaching until 1952. On the *Recommendations for Graduation* dated June 20, 1953, Don clearly signs his name as Don K. Williams Principal. So he is there in 1953 When seventeen eighth graders graduated on June 11, 1953 including James Henry Heflin, Jim Moore, Darrell Dean Richardson, and Betty Johnson. He is also listed as a Buck Mountain School Teacher by the *Bulletin Board* in 1951 although Buck Mountain had already lapsed into Bridgeville School in 1946.

Mr. Grady, Mr. Larsen, Mrs. Thatcher Larsen, Mrs. Fearrien, Mr. Mullan, Jessica Springer, Laurie Church, Dana Johnston, Marty Tavares, Angel Church, Joyce Church, Mrs. Rice, Ms. Mullan, Lori Sheline, Mrs. Grady and Julie Hague-Gray. August 17, 2024.

[50] The *History of Humboldt County Schools* lists her as Eva Stall. But, *Former Bridgeville Teachers* by Janice Crane has her name as Eva Stahl in all instances.

[51] The *History of Humboldt County Schools* lists her as Lovata Davis. But, *Former Bridgeville Teachers* by Janice Crane has her name as Lovesta D. Davis in all instances

[52] The *History of Humboldt County Schools* lists her as Leila Brant. But, *Former Bridgeville Teachers* by Janice Crane has her name as Leila E. Brandt in all instances. Former students, such as Bill May, also spell her name Brandt.

[53] From an interview at Chalk Mountain Ranch May 8, 2018.

[54] William never liked the nicknames "Bill" or especially "Billy" so in second grade he started writing William on all his school papers, even though it was longer.

[55] The *History of Humboldt County Schools* lists him as J. R. McWilliams and begins teaching in 1954, skipping 1955 and teaching again in 1956.. But, *Former Bridgeville Teachers* by Janice Crane has him listed as teaching third and fourth grades in 1955 as Lenox R. McWilliams and teaching upper grades and being the principal in 1956 being listed as L. R. McWilliams.

[56] Les Barnwell interview at Chalk Mt. Ranch May 8, 2018.

[57] From left to right Jean McCall, Shirley Watson, Juanita Mullenix, Bonnie Crabb, Suzanne May, Doreen Ferguson, Verna Lee Ferguson, unknown.

[58] Personal email to Virginia Howard Mullan from Rodney Jones December 25, 2003.

[59] The only reference Virginia Howard Mullan found on Boyd was in the PTA Binder from this year in the attendance section after the name Hattie Boyd was "teacher."

[60] *Humboldt Historian* Winter 2014 page 34.

[61] *Bulletin Board* May 1, 1965. No. 5. This was part of a much longer article (11 paragraphs) in which Mr. Burdick writes about his P.E. program, including describing his favorite exercise: "the student in starting position makes a hard, tight fist, pushes out with his arms and begins to roll-slowly at first-his arms back and forth." Page 7.

[62] *Bulletin Board* May 1, 1965. No. 5. This was part of a longer piece on page 8.

[63] *Bulletin Board* February 1969. No. 3. This was part of a longer piece on Page 2.

[64] *Bulletin Board* December 1968. No. 2. This was part of a longer piece on both page 2 and page 4.

[65] *Bulletin Board* February 1969. No. 3. Page 2.

[66] *Bulletin Board* January 1972. No. 3.

[67] Lola's great grandparents were Anne and Samuel Adams (Samuel Adams of Bridgeville: not one of the Founding Fathers!).

[68] *Humboldt Beacon* article September 1, 1983

[69] *Humboldt Beacon* article September 1, 1983.

[70] This information is from an undated *Times Standard* article from the late 1980s so this information could be off a year or two.

[71] Teacher list from *Humboldt Beacon* in Fortuna, CA. Tuesday, May 20, 1986 page 11.

[72] *Bridgeville Blazers Hall of Flame* 1990-1991.

[73] Flyer put out by Humboldt County Office of Education.

[74] Pam Walker interview in Carlotta, May 2, 2018.

[75] Ibid.

[76] From a *Monthly Board Report* 1993. For several years the staff was required to submit a written report to the Bridgeville School Board summarizing their activities each month. They were also required to attend School Board Meetings on a rotating basis, host the meeting in their classrooms, and give an oral report about current activities.

[77] Ibid.

[78] *Blazer News* Volume 2, Edition 7. Bridgeville School June 15, 1994.

[79] When the Community Center was eventually built next to the office and the new parking lot (a good picture for this is on page 87.) they found huge rotten logs when they began digging. Someone called Jessie Wheeler to ask if she knew what they were from. "Of course," she said, "This is where the Bridgeville Mill log pond was." The author spoke to alumni from back in the day that said they used to enjoy standing on the porch of the old school (page 29) and watch the logs splash when they were unloaded into the pond.

Former students in Ms. Mullan's class standing from left to right: Jessica, Mike, Jessica, Jesse, Brandon, Ms. Mullan, Amanda, Leslie, Samantha, Yana and Tiffany. Kneeling from left to right: Joe, Barry, Angel, Michaelyn, Marcie, Joann and Leah.

[80] Board Report.

[81] Staff verified by State School registers August 28, 1999-June 14, 1996.

[82] Staff list from the year book and verified by State School registers August 26, 1996-June 12, 1997.

[83] Staff verified by State School registers August 25, 1997-June 12, 1998 and 1998 Yearbook (which was really well done with great labels!!!! Way to go Dona Blakely!)

[84] Staff verified by State School registers August 31, 1998-June 17, 1999.

[85] Bridgeville School 1999-2000 Student-Parent Handbook. Printed by Humboldt County Office of Education August 1999. Staff list also verified with State School Registers August 30, 1999-June 15, 2000.

[86] 2009 California Education Code - Section 1920-1924 :: Article 15. Emergency Schools. EDUCATION CODE SECTION 1920-1924.

[87] The *History of Humboldt County Schools* does not include Mrs. Mowery as a teacher at Bridgeville. This information comes from an original form of Recommendations for Graduation dated April 23, 1948 from Bridgeville Emergency School. These were part of the records sent to Bridgeville School when the County Office put their records on microfilm in 1990.

[88] From a series of interviews conducted at Dorothy's Nursery on Wilder Road in Carlotta. Virginia Howard Mullan interviewer. 1992.

[89] *History of Humboldt County Schools*, Volume IV page 2
[90] From *History of Humboldt County Schools* Volume IV.
[91] Ibid.
[92] From an interview with Jessie Wheeler in Eureka 2018.
[93] From an interview recorded by Amanda Hunt and Debbie Bowman in Mr. Grady's Classroom. 1985.
[94] From an interview with Ruth Moorehead French recorded by Tommy Hall in Ms. Mullan's Classroom. 1985.
[95] From an interview recorded by Amber Totten and Courtney Lee in Ms. Mullan's Classroom. 1985.
[96] Interview with Les Barnwell at his ranch, 2018.
[97] *History of Humboldt County Schools*, Volume IV page 37 and comparing the maps on page 90.
[98] Interview with author in Fortuna on December 8, 2018.
[99] Elva Shaw's account in the *Humboldt Historian* May-June 1983
[100] Elva Shaw's account in the *Humboldt Historian* May-June 1983
[101] *Humboldt Standard.* Friday, January 21, 1928.
[102] *History of Humboldt County Schools*, Volume II page 37.
[103] According to *Ink Wells and School Bells* page 89 Irene Fredrickson was the teacher in 1905.
[104] Her father died near Iaqua in 1906.
[105] Elva Shaw's account in the *Humboldt Historian* May-June 1983.
[106] Verna I. Pederson. Private family services were held Friday for Verna I. Pederson who died April 2, 1987, in Eureka. She was a resident of Eureka. Mrs. Pederson retired from the Poultry Producers of Northern California in 1967. Born in Iaqua, she taught school in a one-room schoolhouse in the mountains during

her early life. She was a member of the pioneer Johnson and Fredrickson families of Kneeland. She was a member of Azalea Shrine No. 47, White Shrine of Jerusalem, and a former member of the Business and Professional Women (B.P.W.)

[107] *Humboldt Standard.* Friday, January 21, 1928.

[108] *Introduction to Community Treasures* by the 3/4 class of Van Duzen.

[109] *Carlotta & Yager Valley the First Hundred Years* page 247.

[110] *Carlotta & Yager Valley the First Hundred Years* page 245.

[111] Redwood Emergency School was located seven miles up Redwood House Road, north of Strong's Station. It was a one room school with an outhouse.

[112] In correspondence to Rowetta Stapp Miller from "Max" Rowley, a past local historian. Graciously provided to the author through emails with local historian Rowetta Stapp Miller.

[113] This is an excerpt from Naida Olsen Gipson's article in the *Humboldt Historian* Summer 2008 page 20.

[114] Gipson, Naida Olsen. "Good Neighbors at Showers Pass." *Humboldt Historian* Winter 2017 Volume 65 #4. Pages 10-17.

[115] This could be an error. Or it could be that she taught during a different season/session at the two schools.

[116] From two separate sources. A letter in 1904 and an interview in 1977. This information is from a summary in the *History of Humboldt County Schools*, Volume II page 48.

[117] *History of Humboldt County Schools*, volume II doesn't list Maude Frost as teaching this year, but the September 1977 issue of the *Humboldt Historian* does.

[118] From conversations Rowetta Miller had with her Aunt Muriel "Sis"Stapp, who was her father's oldest sister. Shared through emails with the author August 18, 2024. Oscar and Cordelia "Dee" Stapp moed from their Wildcat homestead, on the northern side of Mad River. They first moved to the Batem (name of the family) place in 1923. Later Oscar and Cordelia purchased the Hagen homestead at Showers Creek. At that time the community was starting to build another school near Coyote Flat.

[119] Alice Jameson in *Ink Wells and School Bells* when talking about Mad River School states, "Nobody even knows there was a school there anymore. When I taught there Darlene Whiting was in first grade."

[120] In correspondence to Rowetta Stapp Miller from "Max" Rowley, a past local historian.

[121] The September 1977 issue of the *Humboldt Historian* refers to it as "Showers Pass School in Hearts Valley" *(no apostrophe)*

[122] *History of Humboldt County Schools*, Volume IV page 2

[123] More information can be discovered in the *Humboldt Historian*

editions Summer 2020 "Heart's (Hart's) Valley School at Showers Pass, Part I (Closed But Memories Linger) and Winter 2020 "Heart's (Hart's) Valley School at Showers Pass, Part II (Closed But Memories Linger), by Rowetta Stapp Miller.

[124] *History of Humboldt County Schools*, Volume II page50 and confirmed by Rowetta Miller in a phone conversation 8/18/2024.

[125] *History of Humboldt County Schools*, Volume IV page 2

[126] *History of Humboldt County Schools*, Volume IV page 2

[127] His last name was spelled differently in different publications and I didn't find any original signature of his to make a determination as to the correct spelling.

[128] *Bulletin Board* November 1956. No. 3. Page 3.

[129] I didn't find this written down anywhere but Sue Gordon who taught at Van Duzen thought the equipment looked the same. Peggy Canale thought the playground equipment looked like what Van Duzen had when she started school there beginning in 1965. The slide looks much shorter than the one that was at Bridgeville School and the swing set doesn't have rings like the Bridgeville School swing set had.

[130] Phone interview July 12, 2024.

Travis Ritter, Gina, Mrs. Fearrien, Tiffany Hunt Neilson, Angel Church, Michaelyn Howard Mullan, and Marcia Mendonca at the All Class Reunion on August 17, 2024.

[131] *History of Humboldt County Schools* lists her name as Helen. I found two instances of documents she signed and both of them with an "e" on the end.

[132] In 2021 Eel River Valley Chapter NSDAR recognized Dr. Doris Niles for her excellent work in science education and instructing local youth. Dr. Niles accompanied Bridgeville School on many "Beach Day" field trips to the South Jetty and helped students identify sea creatures and beach plants. There is also a walking trail named in her honor in 1992 next to Peninsula School near Samoa.

[133] Prairie Johnston also attended the California State Science Fair when she was a freshman in high school.

[134] Information and format provided by Jessica Springer, Administrative Assistant January 10, 2025.

[135] Mrs. Rice, although some years part time, worked at Bridgeville School for 24 years. She was an excellent teacher, 4-H leader, cub scout leader, and basketball coach. She volunteered to judge science fair projects for Bridgeville & Jacoby Creek Schools. She held may overnight field trips to her ranch for Bridgeville School girls. When Mike Grady started at Bridgeville he said that Gordon Crane basically ran the school. He built bookshelves, turn in baskets, and other teacher requested items. Mr. Crane kept everything at Bridgeville in good working order. Mr. Grady worked at Bridgeville for 17 years. Mr. Grady coached football, softball, and basketball before it was ever a paid position. He stayed late with students who needed extra help, before there were "after school programs." Mr. Grady helped new and transfer teachers become better teachers by working with them outside of school time. Mrs. Cathey worked at Bridgeville for 19 years and wrote many grants to improve both the school facilities and teaching equipment. She volunteered as a science fair judge both at Bridgeville and the Humboldt County Science Fair. She loved her students and staff. Students enjoyed her hot tub.

Men and women who attended Bridgeville School: Josh Gatlin, Ryan Samuelson, Tonde Razooly, and Daniel Mendez with Ms. Mullan, October 2024.

Clockwise: Ms. Mullan posing with former students, (circa 2021-2024) who attended Bridgeville School in their youth: Joann, Tonde, Tiffany, Daniel, Emily, Patricia, Elizabeth, Michaelyn, Anora, Matt and Ren.

Clockwise: Sixth through eighth grade in 1990-1991 school year. Saundi Phillips
and kids when Dan Phillips (no relation) came to Bridgeville School in 2020 and told
us about his job at Hulu. Dan Phillips is a Bridgeville School alumnus who had six
students in his eighth grade class. In 2020 Dan won the Cal Poly Humboldt Distin-
guished Alumni Award. That was the year after Ms. Joyce Church, also an alumnus,
was awarded the Franz Bakery teaching award for excellence in teaching. Using
pattern blocks during math instruction, grade class. The softball team; more volleyball
players; Mrs. Cathey.

In 2014 Virginia Howard Mullan and Mike Mullan were honored with a "Mullan's
Garden" in front of the office at Bridgeville School. It is seen above in a picture from
2023. Pam Walker was honored the same year in an area by the kitchen. Unfortunate-
ly, her rock was cracked over the years, seeing a lot more foot traffic on the way to
lunch each day.

MIKE GRADY
Principal

BRIDGEVILLE SCHOOL
Bridgeville, California
1990-1991

MRS. MULLAN-Mr. COOPER
Grades 6-7-8

FRONT ROW: Jacob Scaife, Chano Cruz, Jeremy Buckner, Mike Brinson, Mike Asbury SECOND ROW: Daniel Bywater, Jessica Gatlin, Jenny Peterson, Sherry Jackson, Ruth Jackson, Addie Faustine, Tiffany Hunt, Jessica Wojcik, Shannon Dresen, Alice Hess THIRD ROW: Mr. Cooper-Teacher, Mr. Grady-Dist. Supt., Robyn Samuelson, Prairie Johnston, Leah Sholine, Monika Little, Yana Sweeney, Samantha Gray, Amber Simmons, Heidi Day, Honey Schmidt, Nichole Christensen, Joyce Church-Aide FOURTH ROW: John Buckner, Danny Foster, Nathan Middleton, Brent Bennett, Jacob Middleton, Matt Christensen, Mike McEnry, Cody Hess, Shawn Day, Mrs. Mullan-Teacher, Cathy Jarvis-Aide NOT PICTURED: Maria Mann-Gugne